David Miller Barbour

The Theory of Bimetallism and the Effects of the Partial

Demonetisation of Silver

on England and India

David Miller Barbour

The Theory of Bimetallism and the Effects of the Partial Demonetisation of Silver
on England and India

ISBN/EAN: 9783337419790

Printed in Europe, USA, Canada, Australia, Japan

Cover: Foto ©Suzi / pixelio.de

More available books at **www.hansebooks.com**

THE

THEORY OF BIMETALLISM

AND

THE EFFECTS OF

THE PARTIAL DEMONETISATION OF SILVER

ON

ENGLAND AND INDIA .

BY

D. BARBOUR,

FINANCIAL SECRETARY TO THE GOVERNMENT OF INDIA .

———•◆•———

CONTENTS.

CHAPTER I.

CHAPTER XX.

PREFACE.

I cannot hope at the present day to present the theory of bimetallism in a form which will attract greater attention than it has hitherto received ; but it has appeared to me to be desirable that the whole theory should be restated for the convenience of those who have not followed the course of discussion of the question in recent years, and that certain popular misapprehensions regarding it should be removed. Moreover, the time has now arrived when the effects of the abandonment of bimetallism by the Latin Union on the welfare of India and of England may profitably be examined. For these reasons I have decided, rightly or wrongly, to place the present work before the public. The views which I express are, of course, my personal views, and must not be supposed to represent the opinions of the Government of India.

The total demonetisation of either gold or silver is an impossibility, and the question of the best method of using two metals as money is, therefore, one of the very greatest importance. I have tried to show that the best results for the whole world will be obtained by using them as money at a fixed ratio to be determined by common consent, and I have taken the opportunity of explaining that the bimetallists do not, as is sometimes supposed, wish to fix the market price of a commodity by law ; the bimetallists merely advocate a system of currency which has the advantage of rendering the market ratio of gold to silver very nearly constant.

When France maintained the bimetallic system, there was no law in the French Code which prevented the holder of either gold or silver from selling it in the open market for what it would fetch.

An examination of the economic facts of the last twelve years leads to the conclusion that there would in any case have been a fall in prices after 1873, due to increased population, increased wealth, increased trade, and increased production of commodities ; but that this fall in prices has been aggravated in countries using the gold standard, and checked, or altogether obviated, in countries using the silver standard by the partial demonetisation of silver.

In so far as this has been the case, the silver countries have unquestionably gained, while the gold countries have lost.

On the other hand, the silver countries that had debts in gold have lost, and so have all persons whose incomes were in silver, but who had incurred obligations payable in gold.

Both silver and gold countries have lost by the additional element of uncertainty introduced into all operations of commerce between such countries, as well as by the check imposed on the flow of capital from gold to silver countries.

It cannot be hoped that the adoption of universal bimetallism would bring back gold prices to their old level, or even prevent the possibility of a fall in future years ; but it would have a material effect in this direction, and would thereby mitigate the evils from which all countries with a gold standard are now suffering.

If bimetallism be not accepted by the nations of the world, every fall in the gold price of silver will be followed by a corresponding decline in the gold prices of commodities, by increased disinclination of capitalists in London to invest money in India, by a reduction of profits, and a general increase of the burden of obligations already contracted in England ; and no man can foresee the time when these evils will cease. A great crash may be expected if the monometallists of France and America show that they possess the courage of their convictions by altogether demonetising silver, and selling the depreciated metal in the open market. It would take many years to obliterate the effects of the calamities which would then be experienced ; and when equilibrium had been at last reached, it would still be in the power of the monometallists to reproduce similar disasters by persuading other nations to demonetise silver, or at any rate to attempt to do so.

To ensure the final overthrow of the monometallic theory, it is only necessary that an attempt should be made to carry it out without reservation ; and it is to be feared that no sufficient remedy for present evils can be expected until some such attempt is made, and until monometallism is felt to be intolerable by the countries with which the final decision between the two systems of currency rests.

Some years ago a writer of eminence laid great stress on the prejudice of "our straightforward English minds" in favour of monometallism, and declared that "the unlikely look" of bimetallism would "have as much or more effect on most English minds than any argument."

He was probably right as to the tendency

of many minds to judge of a thing by its "un-likely look, " rather than by argument ; but there are certain facts which even the most "straightforward English minds" will find it difficult to reject on account of their "unlikely look."

Between 1873 and 1884 the value of the foreign trade of England, measured by her standard of value, decreased by ·6 per cent ; in the same period the value of the foreign trade of India, measured by the Indian silver standard, increased by $57\frac{1}{2}$ per cent, and during this time there was no depreciation of silver in India as compared with commodities.

The following table shows the price of wheat in periods of seven years, from 1861 to 1881, in England and in the three chief wheat-producing provinces of India, and also the average price of wheat in 1882-83-84 in both countries :—

PRICE OF WHEAT.

Period.	England, shillings per quarter.	India, rupees per 1,000lbs.
1861—67 ...	50·25	20·7
1868—74 ...	55·25	24·9
1875—81 ...	46·83	23·6
1882—84 ...	40·75	22·7

The average price of wheat in England in 1882-83-84 was less than the average price of wheat during the preceding 21 years by 19·7 per cent. The average price of wheat in India fell only 17 per cent. If the figures of 1885 were compared with those of the period 1861 to 1881, the contrast would be still more striking, as wheat in England has fallen far below the average of 1882-84, while its price in India

remains almost the same. The English farmer
might accept the fall with the less regret if he
thought the English people had gained by having cheap bread ; but the gain is unreal, in so
far as all the products of English industry
have experienced a similar fall—in other words,
in so far as the fall in price is due to the appreciation of gold.

⋅ Nor is there any reason to suppose that the
fall in gold prices is only temporary, or that
we have yet reached the lowest limit. The
diagrams at the end of Chapter XVII show
the course of prices in England according to
the index numbers of the *Economist* from 1845-
50 to 1873, and also from 1873 to 1885, as
well as the prices of silver during the same
periods.

From 1845-50 to 1873, while the world still
retained the advantages of bimetallism, the
range of gold prices in England was indepen-
dent of the prices of silver. Since 1873 the
course of prices has been steadily downwards,
and both the general fall in prices and the
temporary fluctuations in prices have been in
almost exact accordance with the rate of exchange between gold and silver.

The only divergence occurs between 1883 and
1884, and is due to the India Office having
temporarily forced down the price of silver in
the beginning of 1883, by placing bills on the
market in unprecedented amounts.

In the language of Mill, gold prices and the
rate of exchange between silver and gold are
connected by a law of causation, and we cannot
doubt that if silver continues to fall relatively
to gold, the gold prices of commodities will also
continue to fall.

Calcutta, 24th November 1885.

THE

THEORY OF BIMETALLISM.

CHAPTER I.

INTRODUCTORY REMARKS.

THE inconvenience of direct barter led in very early times to the use of money, and the first substance used to discharge, in some degree, the functions of money was, no doubt, one that was in general request, not perishable, and divisible without destruction or impairment of value. Early use of money.

A man who had surplus wheat or any other perishable commodity, found it convenient to exchange it for iron or copper, although he had no immediate use for these metals, because the demand for iron or copper was so general and so steady that at a future period he could safely calculate on being able to get the same weight of wheat, or an equal value of other commodities, for the iron or copper which he accepted in exchange for wheat.

The primary conditions on which the use of any substance as money depends are that the community should be willing to receive it freely in exchange for commodities, and that its value in exchange for commodities should not be liable to serious depreciation. *Primary conditions on which the use of any substance as money depends.*

Iron, copper, salt, and many other commodities have been used as money, and in some *Superiority of silver and gold as money.*

places are still so used ; but the superiority of silver and gold over other substances for use as money has long been established and is beyond question.

The causes which have led to gold and silver being generally accepted as the material of the metallic currency of civilised nations, are well known and need not be repeated.

Not essential that money should possess intrinsic value. Although the money of the civilised world by a natural process came to be coined gold and silver, it will be obvious from what has been said regarding the conditions on which the use of money depends, that it is not essential that the currency should be composed of a substance possessing intrinsic value.

A farmer will be willing to sell his horse for mere tokens, if he knows that the tokens will be readily accepted by those from whom he may afterwards wish to purchase commodities, and if he knows that the tokens will be so limited in quantity as not to lose their value in exchange for commodities.

Inconvertible paper currencies. Consequently we find that inconvertible paper currencies have frequently come into existence. The Government of a country has found itself in a position to compel the people of that country to accept paper tokens, and has forced them into circulation.

No such currency is, however, of any value for the final settlement of balances between two nations. Inconvertible paper may be taken in a foreign country, but only on the understanding that it can be exchanged in the country of origin for something which possesses intrinsic value.

Inferiority of an inconvertible paper currency. For the reason just stated an inconvertible paper currency is inferior to a metallic currency ; but the chief and fatal objection to it is the impossibility of feeling certain that the issue of inconvertible paper money will be so limited as to prevent depreciation.

The farmer can sell his horse for sovereigns in full hope that three months afterwards he will be able to buy another horse, equally good, for the same sum. If, however, he parts with his horse in exchange for tokens, and if the Government afterwards largely increases the issue of tokens,—and Governments are at times very strongly tempted to do so,—he may find that it will take twice as many tokens to purchase another horse, or, in other words, that he has sold his horse in exchange for what turns out to be only half the price he must pay for an equally good horse.

Inconvertible paper money is obviously the cheapest form of currency, but in spite of its economy all nations are anxious to possess a currency which possesses intrinsic value. They find it much safer to trust to the natural laws which regulate the production of the precious metals than to rely upon the wisdom and moderation of the best Government.

All nations desire to possess a currency which has intrinsic value.

Although the use of money is economised by credit, and although nations have from time to time had recourse to an inconvertible paper currency, the legal tender money of the civilised world is essentially gold and silver, and, so far as can be foreseen, will continue to be gold and silver.

Gold and silver will continue to be the metallic money of the civilised world.

Some nations have a gold currency, others a silver currency, others again a currency which is partly silver and partly gold ; it is obviously of great importance that the material of the currency should be employed in the manner which will give the best results for the whole world.

CHAPTER II.

Gold and silver owe their value mainly to their use as money.

GOLD and silver owe almost the whole of their value to the fact that they can be converted into and used as money.

If gold and silver were absolutely excluded from the currency of the world, their value would be greatly reduced, if it did not almost entirely cease to exist; and if either gold or silver were largely excluded from the currency of the world, the value of the metal so excluded would experience a very great fall.

Annual production of gold and silver in the world from 1849 to 1883.

For convenience of reference I give here estimates of the total annual production of gold and silver from 1849 to 1883.

The production of gold from 1849 to 1875 is given on the authority of Tooke and Newmarch and the *Economist*; the production of silver from 1852 to 1875 on the authority of Sir Hector Hay. The figures for both metals from 1876 to 1883 are those given by the Secretary of the Treasury of the United States.

The figures showing the production of silver in 1849, 1850, and 1851 are taken from an estimate by the American Bureau of Statistics. The value of the production of silver in the later years is its value according to the former ratio between gold and silver, and without allowing for the relative depreciation of silver in recent years.

Year.	Gold.	Silver.	Total.
	£	£	£
1849 ...	5,420,000	9,000,000	14,420,000
1850 ...	8,890,000	8,900,000	17,790,000
1851 ...	13,520,000	8,700,000	22,220,000
1852 ...	27,030,000	8,120,000	35,150,000
1853 ...	28,080,000	8,120,000	36,200,000
1854 ...	28,280,000	8,120,000	36,400,000
1855 ...	30,240,000	8,120,000	38,360,000
1856 ...	32,250,000	8,130,000	40,380,000
1857 ...	27,645,000	8,130,000	35,775,000
1858 ...	24,411,000	8,130,000	32,541,000
1859 ...	21,458,000	8,150,000	29,608,000
1860 ...	18,683,000	8,160,000	26,843,000
1861 ...	22,454,000	8,540,000	30,994,000
1862 ...	22,118,000	9,040,000	31,158,000
1863 ...	20,115,000	9,840,000	29,955,000
1864 ...	18,996,000	10,340,000	29,336,000
1865 ...	20,254,000	10,390,000	30,644,000
1866 ...	21,720,000	10,145,000	31,865,000
1867 ...	20,700,000	10,845,000	31,545,000
1868 ...	19,514,000	10,045,000	29,559,000
1869 ...	21,283,000	9,500,000	30,783,000
1870 ...	19,050,000	10,315,000	29,365,000
1871 ...	21,793,000	12,210,000	34,003,000
1872 ...	17,569,000	13,050,000	30,619,000
1873 ...	21,946,000	14,050,000	35,996,000
1874 ...	19,880,000	14,300,000	34,180,000
1875 ...	20,353,000	16,100,000	36,453,000
1876 ...	23,400,000	20,100,000	43,500,000
1877 ...	23,400,000	16,600,000	40,000,000
1878 ...	24,400,000	19,500,000	43,900,000
1879 ...	22,300,000	19,800,000	42,100,000
1880 ...	21,900,000	19,900,000	41,800,000
1881 ...	21,200,000	21,000,000	42,200,000
1882 ...	20,300,000	22,600,000	42,900,000
1883 ...	19,300,000	23,400,000	42,700,000

The reader will recollect that no estimate of the world's production of gold or silver can pretend to more than a very moderate degree of accuracy. *Estimates of production cannot be made absolutely accurate.*

Thus it will be seen that the table above indicates a large increase in the production of both gold and silver for 1876. This apparent increase is no doubt due chiefly to the fact that the figures for years subsequent to 1875 are taken from a different authority.

Extent to which gold and silver discharge respectively the duty of money.

It might at first sight appear that the extent to which gold and silver discharge, respectively, the duties of money, could be determined by ascertaining the ratio which the total amount of silver circulating as coin bears to the total amount of gold circulating as coin, but it would probably give a more accurate result if we could compare the total quantities of gold and silver either used as coin, or hoarded in view to being turned into coin in case of need.

Silver and gold hoarded as a reserve discharge, in one sense, the duty of money.

In consequence of their use as money, gold and silver are very largely hoarded, especially in the East; and as it is assumed that gold and silver can always be converted into coin, or will fetch their full value in exchange for coin, the person who hoards them is often content to hoard them in the form of uncoined bullion. Though not hoarded in the form of coin, they are hoarded as representatives of value; and if other metals were substituted as money for gold and silver, the new metals would have to supply the amount required for hoarding. It is, therefore, fair to say that not only the silver or gold which is circulating as coin, but also the silver or gold which is hoarded with a view to being made into coin in case of need, is performing the duty of money.

Comparison of the relative quantities of gold and silver in the hands of man indicates with sufficient accuracy the extent to which they respectively discharge the duties of money.

It is impossible to say what amount of gold and silver is hoarded as a reserve against a time of distress, and what amount of bullion is used simply to produce articles of luxury, and without any intention of its being thrown into the currency in a time of pressure; as we are unable to determine the relative amounts of gold and silver which are used as coin, and for the purpose of hoarding we must be content to compare the relative amounts of the two metals which are believed to be in the hands of man. The conclusion at which we shall arrive in this way will be sufficiently accurate for the purpose we have in view.

The amount of gold and silver in the hands of man in 1492 was only a fraction of the amount in existence at the present day; but on the discovery of America very valuable mines of gold and silver came to be worked, and it is estimated that from 1493 to 1848 as much as 1,200 millions sterling of silver was produced, and rather more than half that amount of gold.

Increased production of gold and silver after the discovery of America.

After 1848 the relative rate of production altered rapidly, and at one period (1853 to 1857) the value of the gold produce was more than three times the value of the silver produce.

Great increase in the production of gold from 1849.

From 1857, however, the amount of the gold produce fell off, and that of the silver increased, so that at the present time the production of silver is somewhat in excess of that of gold, though if we allow for the depreciation of silver in value relatively to gold, the value of the silver and gold produced every year appears to be very nearly equal.

Falling off in in the production of gold after 1857.

The total amount of gold and silver in existence at the present day cannot, of course, be accurately known; but, according to Tooke and Newmarch, in 1850 there was in existence $15\frac{1}{2}$ millions of pounds (troy) of gold, and $374\frac{1}{2}$ millions of pounds (troy) of silver. Gold being at that date worth $15\frac{1}{2}$ times its weight of silver, it follows that the value of the gold was to the value of the silver, nearly, as 5 to 8, or, in other words, silver discharged eight-thirteenths, and gold five-thirteenths, of the duty of metallic money.

Tooke and Newmarch's estimate of quantity of gold and silver in the hands of man in 1850.

Ernest Seyd's estimate of the q u a n tity of gold and silver coin in exis- tence in 1871. Ernest Seyd calculated that in 1871 there existed 750 millions sterling of gold in the form of coin and bars held by banks and in the mar- ket, and 649 millions sterling of silver held in the same form. These figures would show that in that year gold discharged rather more than one-half of the whole duty of money, but it should be recollected that they do not include sums hoarded, and I have little doubt that there is more silver hoarded than gold.

Dana Harton's estimate of the stock of gold and silver in 1876. Mr. Dana Horton has estimated that in 1876 the total stock of gold in the hands of man was £1,100 millions, and of silver £1,500 millions. This calculation would show that in 1876 silver did rather less than eight-thirteenths of the duty of money, and that gold did rather more five-thirteenths.

The total production of gold and silver from 1877 to 1883 has been, according to the table already given, £152,800,000 and £142,800,000 respectively, the gold showing a tendency to decrease, and the silver to increase.

Esti m a t e of the stock o f gold and silver in 1883. If we take Mr. Dana Horton's figures for 1876 as our starting point, and place the total loss of the precious metals from all causes at 4 millions of gold and 6 millions of silver yearly, we find that the quantities of gold and silver in the hands of man at the end of 1883 were, in round numbers, 1,224 millions and 1,600 mil- lions sterling, respectively.

The Director of the United States Mints has estimated the gold coinage of the civilised world at 3,943 millions of dollars, and the sil- ver coinage at 2,755 millions of dollars; the Director's figures do not include China, where the currency is silver. Bearing this fact in mind, and recollecting also that more silver than gold is hoarded, we cannot doubt that at least one-half of the whole duty of gold and silver as money is discharged by silver alone—even after making an allowance for the present relative depression of silver.

At least one-half the duty of metallic money is discharged by silver alone.

CHAPTER III.

Effect of entirely demonetising silver would be disastrous.

THE conclusion at which we have arrived in Chapter II regarding the relative importance of gold and silver as the medium of exchange, and which is substantially not open to question, enables us to form some conception of what would be the effect of entirely demonetising silver and substituting gold.

This change would not, of course, affect the total wealth of the world. The land would be as productive, and human industry as efficient as before, but silver would practically cease to have any value, while gold would have doubled in value. In other words, property worth from 1,200 to 1,500 millions sterling would have been transferred from the pockets of one class to those of another. Nor would this change, gigantic as it is, represent the whole of the facts ; all debtors would have their debts doubled, while their creditors would gain in a corresponding degree.

No practicable adjustment would render such a change equitable.

To make any such change in the currency of the world equitable, it would be necessary to take from every human being one-half of the gold he possessed, and to transfer it in appropriate quantities to the holders of silver, to reduce all gold coins to half their former weight, and to substitute for silver coins gold ones containing half as much gold as equivalent gold coins would have contained before the demonetisation of silver. All obligations contracted before the change would in the same way require to be adjusted with reference to the new and increased value of gold.

The operation is one that could not be carried out and that will never be attempted, but what has been stated will enable the reader to form some conception of the disasters which must ensue if gold be very much more largely employed as coin than silver. It would, roughly speaking, be fair and in accordance with the present position of gold and silver that half the nations of the world should use silver and half of them gold as metallic money. If two-thirds of the nations took to gold and left one-third with silver, the evils would be enormous ; if three-fourths chose gold, the evils would be still greater ; and if the whole world chose gold to the exclusion of silver, the evils would be such as I have already indicated.

I have stated extreme cases in order to illustrate the evils of change, but there are many intermediate courses involving only minor degrees of loss. For instance, six-tenths of the nations might adopt gold, leaving four-tenths to silver ; and the nations who adopted gold as their standard might, to a greater or less extent, use silver for a subsidiary coinage.

It cannot, however, be too strongly stated that any material change in the amount of duty as money discharged by gold and silver involves an unfair transfer of property from one class to another. If gold is called on to discharge heavier duties than before, it will rise in value, and silver, having less duties to discharge, will fall. All holders of gold will gain, all holders of silver will loose ; all gold debtors will loose, all gold creditors gain ; all silver debtors gain, all silver creditors loose.

Essential injustice of any change in the extent to which gold and silver discharge respectively the duties of money.

Gold countries would probably suffer more from a partial demonetisation of silver than would silver countries. It might be thought that the countries with a gold coinage would gain and those with a silver coinage loose when gold was called on to discharge a heavier share of the duties of money ; but it is very doubtful whether the balance of disadvantage would not be on the side of the countries using gold. The gain of the gold countries would lie in the fact that, internationally, their coin would be worth more than before, and the silver countries would lose from the opposite cause. On the other hand, the gold countries would suffer from a contracting currency and the silver countries from an expanding currency, and the evils which attend a contraction of the currency are much greater than those which follow its expansion.

Great authorities hold that the whole world will probably suffer in future from a contracting currency. If this be the case, the partial demonetisation of silver would be a distinct gain to countries with a silver standard, and a distinct loss to countries with a gold standard.

Complete demonetisation of either gold or silver now generally admitted to be impossible. The complete demonetisation of either gold or silver is absolutely impossible, and this conclusion is now almost universally accepted, although twenty or thirty years ago, when the production of gold was so much in excess of that of silver, there were eminent authorities who held that silver might be demonetised in favour of gold, and others who held that gold must be demonetised to prevent the indefinite depreciation of the currency.

Remarkable change of opinion shown by the three Monetary Conferences held at Paris. The course of public opinion on this question is very clearly indicated by the proceedings of the three Monetary Conferences held at Paris in 1867, 1878 and 1881.

The first Conference had for its object the adoption of a uniform and universal coinage. The importance of a universal monetary unit was exaggerated in its deliberations, and it consequently advocated a gold standard, supplemented temporarily with silver.

The Conference of 1878 came to exactly the opposite conclusion, and declared that it was "necessary to maintain in the world the monetary functions of silver as well as those of gold," while leaving to each State to choose either gold or silver, or both, as the material for its currency.

The Commissioners who represented the British Government at the Monetary Conference of 1878 were permitted to attend only on the express understanding that the question to be submitted to the Conference was not an open one, so far as the United Kingdom was concerned, and that England would in no way depart from the policy which she had pursued for the previous sixty years ; or, in other words, that she was determined to maintain the gold monometallic standard.

The English Commissioners in their Report presented to Parliament, while declaring that they were of opinion that the impossibilities of establishing a bimetallic system by common agreement for all the world were so obvious that it was not worth while urging the matter, nevertheless gave it as their opinion that " a single gold standard throughout the world would be a false utopia, and that further steps in that direction might tend to produce incalculable disasters to the commerce of the world." They considered that the aim of the various States should be " to keep silver in the position which it occupies as the partner or

Margin notes:

The Conference of 1867 recommended a universal gold standard.

The Conference of 1878 came to an exactly opposite conclusion.

The Commissioners who represented Great Britain at the Conference of 1878 were only allowed to attend on the understanding that the monetary question was not an open one as regards the United Kingdom.

Yet the British Commissioners expressed a strong opinion against any further demonetisation of silver.

natural ally of gold in all parts of the world where it might be possible to do so," and "that a campaign undertaken against silver would be exceedingly dangerous, even for the countries who have given a position as legal tender only to gold."

"Nothing surely would create greater disorders in the economic situation, and produce a more disastrous crisis, than a general effort on the part of all States to rid themselves of their silver at the same time."

Considering the position in which the Commissioners were placed, no stronger testimony could be given to the impossibility of demonetising silver.

Impossibility of completely demonetising silver acknowledged at the Conference of 1881

In the Monetary Conference of 1881 the impossibility of demonetising silver was practically admitted to be beyond question.

CHAPTER IV.

OF THE USE OF TWO METALS AS MONEY.

It has been shown in the preceding chapter, both by argument and on the basis of authority, that gold and silver must continue to be used as money unless we are prepared to accept a social cataclysm. It remains to consider in what way the functions of money can best be discharged by the use of two metals.

In what way can two metals be used as money to the best advantage?

There are many ways in which two metals might be used as money. For instance, one set of countries might use one metal, and another set of countries might use the other metal. Or coin might be made to consist of the two metals mixed in a definite poportion. Or the two metals might, as some allege, circulate side by side at a ratio fixed by law, and the ratio might either be fixed once for all, or altered from time to time. There are doubtless other ways in which two metals might be used as money; but in the present day those persons who occupy themselves with the question of the use of gold and silver as money fall naturally into two parties. One party contends that it is possible to use both metals as money, a fixed ratio being, for certain purposes, established by law between them when coined into money; and that it is expedient, if not absolutely necessary so to use them; the other party contends that a fixed ratio between the two metals is an impossibility, both in theory and in practice, and that each country can and should use one only of the

There are various methods of using two metals as money.

But the practical question of the present day refers to the possibility of using the two metals, indifferently, at a fixed ratio.

metals as its standard, the ratio of exchange between the two metals being left to adjust itself by the operation of natural laws.

For all practical purposes it will be sufficient to deal only with the question in dispute between these two parties.*

The problems connected with questions relating to the currency are so complex in their nature that it will be best to begin the attack on them in the simplest form to which they can be reduced. This course has the sanction of Mill, who observed that " on a subject so full of complexity as that of currency and prices, it is necessary to lay the foundation of our theory in a thorough understanding of the most simple cases, which we shall always find lying as a groundwork or substratum under those which arise in practice."

Illustration of the effect of using the metals separately as money in two different countries. Let us, then, suppose that there are but two nations in the world, living side by side, and with a population of one million souls in each. Let us further suppose that the population of each increases at the rate of 10,000 per annum, and that the aggregate wealth increases exactly in the ratio of the population. Let us also suppose that one nation uses a metal which we shall call *A*, and the other a metal which we shall call *B*, as money, and that the quantity of metal *A* and metal *B* produced is just sufficient to increase the currencies of the two countries in exact proportion to their growth in population and in wealth, and that the two nations are, so

---

* I have not thought it necessary to consider a proposal which has recently been discussed, namely, to fix a ratio between gold and silver as a temporary measure, and to vary it, by authority, from time to time according to the state of the market. This system would not remove the evils from which we now suffer, would be found intolerable in practice, and is unnecessary, since if the ratio were once fixed for the world, it would never require to be altered.

far as regards their economic conditions, in a perfectly stationary state, everything increasing in exact proportion to the increase of population.

For the sake of simplifying the problem, we will further suppose that none of the metal used as money is lost, wasted, or employed in the arts.

We will also suppose that one of these nations has got currency of 10 coins of metal *A* per head, or 10 million coins in all. As the population increases at the rate of 10,000 per annum, and as everything in the country increases in exactly the same ratio, it is clear that an addition to the currency of 100,000 (10,000 × 10) coins should be made yearly if prices are to remain the same.

In other words, the production of metal *A* should be just sufficient to supply 100,000 coins yearly.

We will suppose the second nation to hold as currency ten times as much of metal *B* as the first nation possesses of *A*, and the metal *B* is only one-tenth as valuable as metal *A*, weight for weight. The second nation will consequently have a currency composed of 100 coins per head, or of 100 millions of coins in all ; and as the increase of population is 10,000 yearly, it will be necessary that the metal *B* should be produced at such a rate as to be able to supply 1,000,000 coins annually.

If the two nations continue to increase in population and wealth as we have supposed, and if the metals from which their coin is made are produced yearly at the rate of 100,000 and 1,000,000 pieces respectively, it is clear that we shall have a state of things in which the purchasing power of coins of metals *A* and *B* will remain perfectly stationary.

Let us now suppose that metal *A* is suddenly found in larger quantites, and that the production rises to 200,000 coins yearly.

If matters had continued in their old course, there would have been 10,100,000 coins at the end of the first year and prices would have been exactly the same as before. But there are actually 10,200,000 coins in existence; and as there is no greater demand for coins than before, it follows that the coins will fall in value. This is owing to the invariable law which regulates demand and supply.

We may assume that the metal *A* continues to be produced in larger and larger quantities until, when the population reaches 2,000,000, the currency, instead of being composed of 20,000,000 coins, is composed of 30,000,000 coins, and three coins are actually doing the work that was formerly done by two coins. In other words, a coin will only purchase two-thirds of what it would formerly have purchased, and the coins composing the currency have become depreciated to the extent of one-third of their former value.

In the other nation, on the contrary, the increase of currency has been exactly proportional to the work it had to do, and prices have remained the same. The one country has experienced a rise in prices due to over-supply of the material of the currency; the other has had the benefit of stationary prices.

Before the increase in rate of production of metal *A* began, one lb. of that metal purchased the same amount of wheat that could be obtained in exchange for 10 lbs. of metal *B*, and one lb. of metal *A* was exchangeable for 10 lbs. of metal *B*.

Under the new conditions, 10 lbs. of metal *B* will still purchase as much wheat as before, while one lb. of metal *A* will only purchase two-thirds of that amount; it follows that one lb. of metal *A* will now exchange for only $6\frac{3}{4}$ lbs. of metal *B*, instead of for 10 lbs.

The result therefore has been that there has been a rise of prices in the first nation, and simultaneously an alteration in the rates at which the two metals exchange.

If we assume that the production of metal *B* has been decreasing while that of metal *A* has been increasing, we get a double effect. Prices will have risen in the country that uses metal *A*, and fallen in the country that uses metal *B*. Both countries will have suffered from variation in prices, and there will have been also a variation in the ratio in which the two metals exchange against each other.

It will readily be understood that prices might rise by one-third in the first country, while they fell by one-third in the second country. The total amount of the two currencies taken together would, in this case, be exactly what it ought to be in order that prices might remain stationary; but one country would have one-third too much, and the other one-third too little, and consequently one country would suffer from a rise and the other from a fall in prices.

At this stage the question naturally arises, whether it would be possible by any means to so arrange matters that the excess in one country should balance the deficit in the other, and that both countries should have the benefit of stated prices.

Is it possible to arrange that the excess production of one metal shall balance the short production of the other?

Assuming, as before, that the population in each country has increased from 1,000,000 to

2,000,000, and that there has arisen an excess of
one-third of the total currency in one country
and a deficiency to the extent of one-third in
the other, we find that the country which ought
to have had 20 millions of A coins has got $26\frac{2}{3}$
millions ; the other country required 200 millions of B coins, but has only got $133\frac{1}{3}$ millions.

An obvious remedy for the variation in prices
in the two countries is that one-third of the
population of the second country should give
up the use of the metal B and use metal A.

If this be done, we shall have $2\frac{2}{3}$ millions of
people with $26\frac{2}{3}$ millions of A coins, or 10 coins
per head, and $1\frac{1}{3}$ millions of people with $133\frac{1}{3}$
millions of B coins, or 100 coins per head. As
these are the amounts per head required by our
hypothesis to maintain equilibrium, prices will
neither rise nor fall in the two countries, and
the coins will interchange at the rate of 1 to 10,
as before.

This can be
done in theo-
ry, by altering
the distribu-
tion of the po-
pulation using
the two me-
tals.
And in any
case the maxi-
mum variation
in price can be
avoided by re-
distribution of
population.

We thus see that if the production of one
metal increases just as much as that of the other
falls, it is possible by a redistribution of the
population using the two metals to bring about
equilibrium in prices.

If the production of one metal fell off and
that of the other remained stationary, it would
not be possible to bring about equilibrium by
any redistribution ; but it would be possible by
redistributing the population to spread the
effect of the excess production over both countries, and in this way to diminish the maximum
amount of the rise in prices. If no redistribution were made, prices would rise in one country
and remain stationary in the other. By redistribution we can reduce the variation in price to
half what it otherwise would have been, but at

the same time we bring double the population
under the influence of the rise.

It is obviously better that the variation in
prices should be reduced in degree by being
spread over the whole world than that the
total rise due to excess production should fall
on a few countries.

The most unfavourable case would arise when
the rate of production of both metals increased
equally or decreased equally at the same time.
In such case no distribution that could be made
would have any effect. But if the rate of production of one metal increased while that of the
other decreased, or if they both rose or both fell
together, but one more rapidly than the other,
it would be possible by a redistribution of the
population using the two metals to reduce the
maximum variation in price due to the rise or
fall in the rate of production of the metals.

In other words, by redistribution of the
population a steadying effect on prices could be
produced in every case but one; and that one
is not likely to occur in practice.

Although it is possible to show that, in
theory, a steadying influence could be exercised
on prices by redistributing the population using
the two metals, it must be admitted that any
such process is out of the question in practice.
Who is to say that the production of one metal
has so increased in reference to the other metal
as to make a redistribution of population desirable? Who is to investigate the thousand
elements that effect price, and to say there is a
general rise or a general fall, and that it is due
to increased or diminished production of one of
the precious metals rather than to some other
cause? And, above all, what probability is
there that any nation would change its currency

In practice,
however, it
would be
found impos-
sible to make
any such re-
distribution.

at the bidding of some authority to which it owed no allegiance, and whose dicta must be of very doubtful correctness ?

It is wholly impossible in practice to re-adjust the currencies of different countries from time to time, so as to assign to each of two metals the exact amount of duty as money which involves the minimum alteration in prices.

CHAPER V.

Two principles which, it has sometimes been said, should regulate the distribution of the countries of the world between gold and silver may now conveniently be noticed. The two principles that have been put forward are—

(1) All rich nations should use gold, and all poor ones silver ; or

(2) All civilised nations should use gold, and all uncivilised nations silver.

Absurdity of certain principles which have been put forward to regulate the distribution of gold and silver money among the nations of the world.

These principles are open to so many objections that it is difficult to deal with them seriously. What is to be done if a rich nation becomes poor, or if an uncivilised nation becomes civilised ?

What will happen if all nations become equally civilised or equally rich ?

Who is to decide with binding authority what nations are rich, and what nations are civilised ? Will not each nation decide for itself whether it is poor or rich ; whether it is civilised or uncivilised ?

Why should a poor nation use silver ? If a nation requires £10,000,'00 as currency, it will have to pay the same for it, whether it chooses gold or silver. There is no economy in using a silver currency rather than a gold one. In either case the currency must be of a certain value, and therefore a silver currency will cost just as much as a gold one.

A silver standard and currency are not cheaper than a gold standard and currency.

Small debts can, no doubt, be most conveniently discharged with silver coins, because gold coins of very small value would be so minute as to be inconvenient to handle, and, presumably, the proportion of small debts is greater in a poor country than in a rich one; but rich countries as well as poor ones find it necessary to issue a subsidiary coinage in silver, copper, or bronze, for the payment of small debts, and a poor country will simply require a larger proportion of these subsidiary coins.

What likelihood is there that a division based on the comparative wealth or degree of civilisation of the nations of the world would permanently coincide with a division based on the relative capacity of gold and silver to meet the demand for an increase of the currency? None whatever.

Other rules also have been prescribed for regulating the use of silver. One is that the nation that has got a gold standard should keep to the gold standard, and the nation that has got a silver standard should keep to its silver standard. Another is that each nation should do exactly as it likes. There is something to be said for the former of these principles; indeed, the only objection to it is that it would confine the effect of over or under production of any metal to half the nations of the world instead of distributing it over the whole world.

The latter principle is the one that now regulates the use of gold and silver by the world. I do not know anything to be said in its favour.

CHAPTER VI.

EFFECT ON PRICES OF USING TWO METALS AS CURRENCY AT A FIXED RATIO.

Can the stability of price that would be given by periodical redistribution of the population using two metals separately as money be obtained in any other way?

It has already been shown that if two metals are in use in different countries as money, the greatest possible stability of price can, in theory, be obtained by an alteration from time to time of the proportion of the total population using each metal; and I have admitted that in practice any such modification is impossible.

Is it possible to devise any practicable means of using the two metals as money which will give the same stability of price that would be obtainable if we could only distribute the two metals at our wish among the populations of the world?

About this question rages the dispute of the monometallists and the bimetallists.

Contention of the bimetallists.

The contention of the bimetallists is that it is possible to declare a fixed ratio of exchange, for certain purposes, between the two metals when used as money, debts being paid at the option of the debtor in coins of either metal, and that the existence of this fixed ratio for the purposes of the currency will control and regulate the market price of the two metals so as to prevent it from varying in any material degree from the fixed legal ratio of the currency.

In order to test the effect on prices of declaring a fixed ratio between the two metals when coined, let us again make the assumptions

Assuming that
the two metals
would circu-
late at the
fixed ratio,
the effect of
bimetallism
would be to
give the maxi-
mum amount
of stability to
prices.

that were made on page 15. We shall then
have, at starting a population of one million
with a currency of 10,000,000 coins of A metal,
and another population of one million with a
currency of the same value, but consisting of
100,000,000 coins of B metal.

Assuming that both countries remain monometallic, we shall have in the next stage a
population of two millions with a currency of
$26\frac{2}{3}$ millions of A coins, being an excess of
$6\frac{2}{3}$ millions of coins, and we shall have another
population of two millions with only $133\frac{1}{3}$
millions of B coins, showing a deficit of $66\frac{2}{3}$
millions of B coins.

At the old ratio of 10 to 1, the $6\frac{2}{3}$ millions
of A coins which are in excess are exactly of
the same value as the $66\frac{2}{3}$ millions of B coins.

If, then, before the rate of production of the
two metals began to vary it had been declared
that the A and B coins were full legal tender at
the ratio of 1 to 10 throughout both countries,
we should, according to the bimetallists, have
had $26\frac{2}{3}$ millions of A coins and $13\frac{1}{3}$ millions of
B coins forming the currency for four millions
of people. The $133\frac{1}{3}$ millions of B coins being
worth $13\frac{1}{3}$ millions of A coins, it follows that the
value of the total currency is 40 millions of A
coins, or, in other words, we have for four
millions of people a currency which is of the
value of 10 coins of A metal per head. This
is the exact amount required by our hypothesis
to ensure stability of price, and we consequently
see that the alternative and optional use of the
two metals as money at a fixed ratio secures
stability of price, provided that the two metals
do actually circulate side by side at that ratio.

CHAPTER VII.

OBJECTIONS COMMONLY RAISED TO THE POSSIBILITY OF TWO METALS CIRCULATING AT A FIXED RATIO.

WE have now got to the very heart of the bimetallic question. Will the two metals circulate side by side at the fixed ratio ?

Can two metals be made to circulate at a fixed ratio ?

Those who oppose the alternative or bimetallic standard say that it is impossible to fix the relative values of commodities by law; for instance, one bushel of wheat cannot by law be made exchangeable for two bushels of oats. The two metals (gold and silver) are commodities ; therefore the ratio of exchange between them cannot be fixed by law.

Objection based on the argument that gold and silver are commodities.

Some hold that under the operation of the rule that bad money tends to drive out good money, the metal that was the more easily produced would gradually oust the other metal, while others declare that the ratio of exchange between two metals must depend upon demand and supply, and cannot be fixed by law.

Objection based on Gresham's Law.

It is also argued that the value of gold and silver must in the long run be determined in the one case by the cost of production of gold at the least productive gold mine that is worked, and in the other case by the cost of production of silver at the least productive silver mine that is worked, and that it is consequently futile to attempt to lay down a fixed ratio for determining the relative value of gold and silver.

Objection based on the law of cost of production.

False impression regarding bimetallism.

Before proceeding to examine these arguments in detail, I wish to correct a misapprehension which has been the cause of a great deal of opposition to bimetallism on the part of persons who have formed their opinions without a careful study of the subject.

The bimetallists do not wish the market price of gold and silver regulated by law.

It is a mistake to suppose that the bimetallists wish to see a law passed which shall fix the market price of gold and silver. No man is to be forced to sell one ℔. of gold for exactly 15½ ℔s.* of silver if he can get more for it, or to be prevented from accepting less than 15½ ℔s. of silver if he is willing to do so. Under the bimetallic system the State simply undertakes to coin both gold and silver freely if brought to it. It also declares that it will accept indifferently, in payment of money due to it, coins of either metal, the relative amounts of coin required to discharge a debt being determined by the fixed ratio. All persons who enter into agreements with the State involving the receipt by them of money, must also be prepared to accept either gold or silver coin according to the fixed ratio; and if two private persons enter into a contract involving the receipt and payment of money without specifying whether payments are to be made in gold or in silver, the person who has a payment to make is given the option of making it either in gold or silver, the quantity in each case being determined by the fixed ratio.

---

* I use the old French ratio of 1 to 15½ for convenience, but there is no magic in the ratio of 1 to 15½ rather than in the ratio of 1 to 10 or 1 to 20. The ratio of 1 to 15½ was the market ratio, or very close to it, in the beginning of the present century; it was adopted as the legal ratio by France, and this decision fixed the market ratio at 1 to 15½ for 70 years.

Bimetallists do not claim that the market price of gold and silver shall be fixed by law. They desire to see the currency regulated in a certain way; and they hold that if this be done the ratio of the market will, for practical purposes, remain unchanged.

They merely wish to see the currency regulated in a certain way, and they hold that the result will be to maintain a constant market ratio between gold and silver.

In connection with this question I would call the reader's attention to what was said in page 4, that the value of gold and silver is almost entirely due to their use as money, and that consequently the relative value of gold and silver depends upon the extent to which the different nations of the world use these metals as currency. If one nation after another decided to demonetise silver and to sell the silver contained in its currency, the value of silver relatively to commodities, and still more so in comparison with gold, could be made to fall to a very small fraction of its present value. On the other hand, if the nations of the world demonetised gold and sold their gold, the value of gold in relation to silver would experience a very great fall.

The value of gold and silver is almost entirely due to their use as money.

In short, we see that the demand for gold or silver is due mainly to the extent to which the legislatures of the different countries decide to use these metals as money, and therefore their relative value is, and must continue to be, regulated by legislation.

The extent of the use of each metal as money depends on legislation. Therefore the relative value of each metal is regulated, in any case, by legislation.

The only question is whether it is better to allow the legislatures to act independently in a haphazard way, making the ratio now this, now that, or whether the legislatures should act in unison, with a full knowledge of the problem, and legislate in such manner as to give the world a constant ratio between gold and silver, if it be possible to do so, and the blessing of prices as stable as it is possible to make them by a judicious management of the currency.

Is it better that the values of gold and silver should be regulated by haphazard legislation or by legislation that has considered the ends at which it should aim?

CHAPTER VIII.

OBJECTIONS TO THE FIXED RATIO BASED ON THE FACT THAT GOLD AND SILVER ARE COMMODITIES.

Danger of using general propositions.

IN taking up the argument based on the contention that gold and silver are commodities, and that consequently the ratio of exchange between them cannot be fixed, I would, in the first place, remind the reader of the dangers that attend the use of general propositions.

Gold and silver, when freely coined into money and made legal tender, are subject to conditions which do not apply to other commodities.

It is bad logic to prove that the ratio of exchange between wheat and barley cannot be fixed by law, to assert that the ratio of exchange between any two commodities cannot be so fixed, and deduce from this general proposition the conclusion that the ratio of exchange between gold and silver cannot be fixed, when in fact by their being declared to be legal tender at a defined ratio, gold and silver are made subject to conditions which do not apply to any other commodities.

What is true of commodities generally is not necessarily true of gold and silver when they are given a status different from that of all other commodities.

And, unquestionably, gold and silver when used as money under a bimetallic system, possess qualities which other commodities do not possess.

I can get into a hatter's and offer him gold or silver coins for a hat, with a firm conviction that he will take them in exchange, and with an equally firm conviction that if I offered him wheat he would not take it. I can pay all my debts in gold or silver coin, offering either so many gold coins or so many silver coins. My creditors would not be bound to take either wheat or barley. I can pay all taxes in gold or silver coin, choosing either metal, and, according as I choose gold or silver, paying either a less or greater weight of metal according to the fixed legal ratio. I could not pay taxes by delivering wheat or barley, nor is there any fixed ratio at which Government would accept them. If I am cast in damages in a suit, I must pay so many gold or so many silver coins, not so much wheat.

I mention these facts to show that though it may be impossible to fix a ratio of exchange by law between wheat and barley, it must not be inferred therefrom that it is impossible to devise currency laws which will, in practice, have the effect of rendering constant the ratio of exchange between two metals forming the basis of the currency.

If gold and silver are freely coined to form the currency of a country, and if they are declared to be a legal tender at a certain ratio, they are thereby made subject to conditions which do not apply to wheat and barley ; and it is impossible to argue that what holds good in the case of wheat and barley must also hold good in the case of gold and silver.

CHAPTER IX.

OBJECTIONS TO THE FIXED RATIO BASED ON
GRESHAM'S LAW.

Bad money tends to drive out good.

LET us now consider the working of the law that bad money drives out good.

It is almost an axiom that if a currency consists of two classes of coins of the same legal value, but of which one class of coins is intrinsically more valuable than the other; and if there is a demand, other than the demand as money, for the material of which the coins are made, the coins which are intrinsically the more valuable will be withdrawn, to a greater or less extent, to supply this demand.

Because outside the currency the good money is the more valuable.

Why is this the case? For the following reasons. The two classes of coins are of equal value as legal tender, in payment of taxes, or debts, or, by law in exchange for commodities. But if any one wishes to use the coins for any other purpose than as money, it is to his advantage to use those which are intrinsically the more valuable. Ten of the inferior coins are just as useful in paying debts as ten of the better coins; but for all purposes not connected with currency, the latter class of coins is the more valuable. Therefore the coin which is intrinsically the more valuable will be withdrawn for purposes not connected with the currency, in preference to the other coin, and the reduction of the total amount of the currency will be met by the introduction of an equal number of the inferior coins. In this way bad coin tends to drive out good, because for other purposes than use as money it is more economical to use the good coin.

I admit that if coins made of different metals are circulating side by side at a ratio fixed by law, and if the cost of production of one of the metals decreases to a greater extent than is consistent with the fixed ratio, the metal which is more cheaply produced will tend to be coined more largely than would otherwise have been the case. If silver and gold coins are legal tender at the rate of 1 to $15\frac{1}{2}$, and if the cost of production would give a ratio of 1 to 17, there will certainly be an increase of the coinage of silver, and a reduction in the coinage of gold.

The effect of this law on a bimetallic currency is to increase the coinage of the metal which for the time being is produced the more cheaply.

The bimetallists, however, contend that if the ratio fell for an instant from $15\frac{1}{2}$ to 1 to a ratio of 17 to 1, there would immediately and *ipso facto* arise an increased demand for silver for coinage and a reduced demand of gold for coinage, and that this increase of demand for silver and decrease of demand for gold would continue until the equilibrium of $15\frac{1}{2}$ to 1 was again brought about.

This increase of coinage means an increased demand, and tends always to maintain the fixed ratio.

It appears to me impossible to doubt that if $15\frac{1}{2}$ ℔s. of silver serve my purpose as well as one ℔. of gold, and if I can exchange one ℔. of gold for 17 ℔s. of silver, I shall never bring my one ℔. of gold to the mint to be coined. I shall prefer to exchange one ℔. of gold for 17 ℔s. of silver ; of the 17 ℔s. of silver I shall take $15\frac{1}{2}$ ℔s. to the mint to be coined, and I shall have saved $1\frac{1}{2}$ ℔s. of silver.

If the ratio fixed by law between the two metals ever ceased in any material degree to be the ratio of the market, the dearer metal would at once be withdrawn from circulation and offered in exchange for the cheaper metal, and this process would go on as long as the divergence in ratio continued. The effect must be to bring about the fixed ratio again, or to withdraw the whole of the dearer metal from the currency.

Under the bi-metallic system either the fixed ratio will be maintained, or the whole of the dearer metal will be withdrawn from the free circulation.

Either, therefore, the whole of the dearer metal will be withdrawn from circulation or the ratio fixed by law between the two metals will become again the ratio of the market. If there existed a great and sustained demand for gold for other purposes than that of currency, it is conceivable that silver might continue at the ratio of 17 to 1 until gold had absolutely ceased to circulate as money, but this result could never come about in practice. Let us

Illustration of the impossibility of any other than the fixed ratio prevailing under a universal bimetallic system.

assume that there is £700,000,000 sterling of gold coin in the world and £700,000,000 sterling of silver coin, and that the annual production of gold and silver is £20,000,000 sterling in each case. Let us further assume that the labour which produced £20,000,000 worth of silver suddenly, owing to the discovery of new and more valuable mines, produces £30,000,000 (at the fixed legal ratio), and that consequently the ratio of the market falls to 1 to 17. Instantly there will be a profit to be made by exchanging gold for silver bullion and bringing the silver to the mint. The £700,000,000 of gold in the currency *plus* the year's production of £20,000,000 would at once compete in exchange for the £30,000,000 of silver just produced ; everybody who owned gold coined or uncoined would hasten to exchange it for silver at the rate of 1 to 17, and would find his profit in paying his debts and taxes at the ratio of 1 to 15½. To suppose that any other ratio than that of 1 to 15½ could be maintained for a single hour when the holders of £720,000,000 of gold were offering it for £30,000,000 sterling of silver at any rate better than 1 to 15½, is absurd.

If both metals are freely coined into legal tender money throughout the world at a fixed ratio, no other ratio of exchange is possible, unless the production of one of the metals should be so overwhelming, and the demand for the other metal for purposes unconnected with the currency so great, that the whole of the scarcer metal is withdrawn from the currency for other purposes.

It is theoretically possible that one metal might be wholly withdrawn from the currency.

Even in the extreme case where one metal entirely drove the other out of circulation, the rise in prices would be less than it would be if we confined the use of silver to certain countries, and gold to other countries. In the latter case the excess supply of silver would not raise prices in the gold-using countries, but it would raise prices to a still higher level in the countries that used silver only, and the increase of price that would result would be higher than if gold and silver had been used in all countries at a fixed ratio and the former metal had been altogether driven out of circulation.

Even in the latter case prices would be more stable than under a monometallic system.

If the currency of the world continued to absorb the total yearly supply of both silver and gold, prices must be higher than if gold had been driven out of circulation and the currency were composed of silver only.

Of course gold might as easily be driven out of circulation by a rise in its cost of production as by a fall in the cost of production of silver; but as we have already seen, the use of the two metals as legal tender coin at a fixed ratio can in no case give a greater variation in prices than the use of one metal, and would practically in all cases give a less variation.

This law of the bad money driving out the good is, therefore, merely the means by which the bimetallic system acts. If the cost of production of one metal decreases relatively to the cost of production of the other metal, the former will be more largely produced, and will tend to exclude the dearer metal, and the increased production of the one and the diminished demand for the other will be regulated by the fixed ratio.

CHAPTER X.

THE exchange ratio of two metals must depend on demand and supply. How then can this ratio be fixed by law?

The answer is simple, and has already been given. Under the bimetallic system the market ratio is not fixed by law. The laws regulating the currency are so framed that the demand is for silver when $15\frac{1}{2}$ lbs. of silver can be obtained for less than one lb. of gold, and that the demand is for gold when more than one lb. of gold can be obtained for $15\frac{1}{2}$ lbs. of silver.

The bimetallic system controls the price of gold and silver by acting on the demand for the two metals.

The law says nothing about the market ratio, but it establishes a currency system, which, by regulating the demand, keeps the market ratio constant. The bimetallic system acts on the market through the law of demand and supply and not in opposition to it.

It is also said that the cost of production at the least-paying mine of each metal must determine its value, and that consequently the law cannot fix the relative values of gold and silver.

I have already shown that under the bimetallic system the law does not arbitrarily fix the relative market price of gold and silver; that it merely legalises a system of currency which, by the operation of natural laws, tends, under certain conditions, to preserve a fixed ratio between gold and silver.

The cost of production is accommodated to the fixed ratio by the extension or limitation of the mines of each metal, as the case may be. In the same way the operation of these laws is such that mines of one or the other metal either cease to be worked, or are extended in such manner as to make the cost of production at the worst-paying mine exactly equal to the value of the metal produced at that mine.

Let us consider again the state of matters assumed to exist in page 16. Ten thousand coins of *A* metal and 100,000 coins of *B* metal are produced at the same cost, and one coin of *A* metal exchanges for 10 coins of *B* metal. Suddenly an invention is discovered which enables the *A* metal to be produced for exactly one-half the labor previously expended on it. One pound of *A* metal would now in ordinary circumstances be worth only 5 lbs. of *B* metal; but the one lb. of *A* metal can be taken to the mint and made into coins which serve the same purpose as ten times the same number of *B* coins. The men who work at producing metal *B* will immediately see that it is more profitable for them to turn their attention to the production of metal *A*. By working a month a miner obtains 10 lbs. of *B* metal; but if he worked at producing *A* metal, he would produce 2 lbs., which would be as effective in paying rent or taxes or in discharging ordinary debts, as 20 lbs. of *B* metal. He will therefore give up producing *B* metal and will turn his attention to producing *A* metal.

In this way the least-paying mines of *B* metal would be abandoned, and new mines (and less-paying ones) of *A* metal would be opened, and this process would necessarily go on until the least-productive *A* mines and the least-productive *B* mines gave exactly the same profit at the fixed ratio of 1 to 10.

The ratio of exchange must depend on supply and demand ; but the demand being, *ex hypothesi*, not a demand for metal *A*, nor a demand for metal *B*, but a demand for metal *A* when the ratio is better than 1 to 10, and a demand for metal *B* when the ratio is worse than 1 to 10, the supply of the two metals necessarily adjusts itself to the ratio of 1 to 10.

The cost of production in the least-valuable mine of each kind of metal will certainly, in the long run, be equal to the value of that metal ; but it is not the cost of production that determines the value, but the relative value which leads to the abandonment of the worst-paying mines of one metal and the opening of mines of the other metal until the relative cost of production at the worst-paying mines of the two metals exactly corresponds with the fixed ratio of exchange.

The metals are legal tender at the fixed ratio of 1 to 10, and (if necessary) the production of one metal will increase and that of the other fall off until this becomes the ratio of the cost of production at the two classes of mines which are least productive.

It is of course conceivable that the fixed legal ratio might not be attained even by the total abandonment of all the mines of one of the metals ; but in that case, if there were no demand, except as money, for the metal which was the more costly to produce, it would simply cease to be produced.

CHAPTER XI.

THE manner by which stability of price, as some hold, is brought about by free coinage of two metals into legal tender money at a fixed ratio, has already been explained; but for the purpose of securing stability of price it is not, under certain conditions, necessary that all countries should coin both metals. The same effect will be produced if a country, or group of countries, with a sufficiently large currency agrees to coin either metal indifferently and to make both kinds of coin legal tender at a fixed ratio, every other country coining one metal only.

Illustration of the effect on prices when some countries are bimetallic and others monometallic.

Let us suppose that there are three countries subject to the conditions assumed to exist in page 16. Each country has a population of 1,000,000, —one country coins A metal only and requires 10,000 coins annually; the second coins B metal only and requires 100,000 coins; and the third coins either A metal or B metal at the ratio of 1 to 10, and requires an addition to its currency every year of the same value as the addition to the currency of each of the other countries.

If we assume the production of A metal to be 15,000 coins anually and of B metal 150,000 coins annually, the first nation will coin 10.000 A coins yearly, the second 100,000 B coins, and the third will coin 5,000 *A* coins and 50,000 *B* coins.

Let us now assume that the production of *A* coins rises to 18,000 yearly, and consider what will happen.

Each nation will add the same amount in value to its currency, and therefore the excess production will be distributed between the first and third nations, and the proportion of the *B* metal coined by the second nation will be increased.

If we distribute the two metals between the three countries on the condition that the currency of each country gets an increment of equal value, we find that the first country must add to its currency 11,000 *A* coins, and the second 110,000 *B* coins, while the third will add to its currency 7,000 *A* coins and 40,000 *B* coins.

In other words, the value of each of the three currencies remains the same, and the rise in prices due to the excess production of metal *A* is equally distributed over the whole set.

The result is therefore the same as if all three nations had been bimetallic instead of two being monometallic, one with *A* metal and one with *B* metal, the third being bimetallic.

If the over-production of *A* metal continued in future years, it will be evident that the third nation would go on absorbing a portion of the surplus and giving up a portion of the *B* metal to the second nation. On the other hand, if over-production of *B* metal took place, the third nation would absorb a portion of the surplus of that metal and would give up a portion of the *A* metal to the first nation.

We thus see that the bimetallic system may be completely carried out although some countries are monometallic, provided there is a country or group of countries which is prepared to coin both metals freely, and to accept them as legal tender at a fixed ratio.

It is an interesting question to determine how long a bimetallic country surrounded by monometallic countries can, unaided, sustain the bimetallic system.

Limitation of the power of a bimetallic country to maintain the fixed ratio when other countries are monometallic.

The answer is simple, and is obvious from the considerations that have been already stated.

A single country can sustain the system so long as its currency is actually composed of both metals.

If one metal becomes so abundant in comparison with the other that the latter is completely driven out of the country which uses the alternative standard, the principle of compensation ceases to act, and the country that was bimetallic becomes practically monometallic.

If the currency of the bimetallic country is totally denuded of one of the metals, the legal ratio ceases to be the market ratio.

The market ratio between the two metals will then cease to be constant, and may vary to any extent.

If the metal which was over-produced ceases to be over-produced, and if over-production of the other metal begins, the bimetallic country, which was denuded of the latter metal, will begin to get it back again as soon as the market ratio returns to the legal ratio.

And it is quite possible that the currency of the bimetallic country might at one time be composed wholly of one metal, and at a future time be composed wholly of the other metal.

Essential condition for the maintenance of the fixed ratio by a single bimetallic country or a group of bimetallic countries.

What is necessary therefore for the proper maintenance of the bimetallic system, when some countries are monometallic, is that the group of bimetallic countries should have a currency so extensive that it will afford complete scope for the play of the two metals according as one or other is over or under-produced, without becoming completely denuded of either metal.

It has happened that different countries have been at the same time bimetallic, but each with a different fixed ratio.

In such cases each metal will drift towards, and be absorbed into, the currency of the country where it is most highly valued, and if the difference in the fixed ratios adopted by different countries is of sufficient magnitude to make it worth while to export coin from one country to another, exportation will take place until at last one of the countries only will hold both metals in its currency, and the ratio established by that nation between the two metals will be the ratio which regulates the market price.

Ultimate result when different countries adopt different ratios.

The United States were at one time bimetallic at 1 to 16, and France at 1 to $15\frac{1}{2}$. The result was that gold was coined in America and that silver tended to flow from America to France. The stream of silver that flowed to France was not of sufficient volume to totally exclude gold from her currency; and the world still retained the benefits of the bimetallic system at the French ratio, namely 1 to $15\frac{1}{2}$, the effect of the American ratio of 1 to 16 being to render the United States for the time practically monometallic.

CHAPER XII.

Possibility of controlling the market by selling or buying at a certain rate.

THE question of the possibility of a bimetallic State surrounded by monometallic States maintaining a fixed ratio may be illustrated in the following manner. Assuming that the ratio of the bimetallic State is 1 to $15\frac{1}{2}$, what that State undertakes to do is this—

(1) Any person who chooses may bring a pound of gold to the mint and have it coined into gold coins, and may then get $15\frac{1}{2}$ lbs. of silver coins in exchange for his gold coins.

(2) Or he may bring $15\frac{1}{2}$ lbs. of silver, and by a similar process exchange it for one pound of gold.

The position is exactly the same as if a merchant came into the open market and offered to all-comers either to give 2 bushels of wheat for 3 bushels of barley, or to give 3 bushels of barley for 2 bushels of wheat.

In the latter case no other ratio than that of 2 to 3 could prevail between wheat and barley.

Let us assume that when the merchant offered these terms of exchange, the market rate was 2 bushels of wheat to $3\frac{1}{2}$ bushels of barley.

As soon as the merchant made his offer, all persons who had barley to sell would resort to him. They would say, " If we can get 2

bushels of wheat for 3 bushels of barley from
this man, why should we give $3\frac{1}{2}$ bushels for
the same amount of wheat in the market?"
As long, therefore, as the merchant's stock of
wheat enabled him to give 2 bushels of wheat
for 3 of barley, no holder of barley would take
less than 2 bushels of wheat for 3 of barley.

And the holder of barley would find it impossible to get more than 2 bushels of wheat,
for if the market rate became $2\frac{1}{2}$ bushels of
wheat to 3 of barley, the holder of wheat
would say, " I will not give $2\frac{1}{2}$ bushels of
wheat for 3 of barley, because I can go to this
merchant and get 3 bushels of barley for 2
bushels of wheat." So long, therefore, as the
merchant had both wheat and barley in his
possession and was prepared to exchange one
for the other at the ratio of 2 to 3, no other
ratio could possibly prevail in the market. If
his stock of either wheat or barley ever became wholly exhausted, he could no longer
make the exchange in the case of the grain
which he did not possess, and would lose his
power of maintaining the ratio of 2 to 3. The
case is exactly analogous to that of a bimetallic
nation surrounded by monometallic nations.

If a merchant is prepared to sell an article to
all-comers at a certain price, no higher price
can prevail in the market; if he is prepared to
buy it at a certain price, no lower price can
prevail. The bimetallic nation is prepared to
buy gold at 1 to $15\frac{1}{2}$, therefore no lower price
for gold can exist in the market; it is prepared
to sell gold at 1 to $15\frac{1}{2}$, therefore no higher
price can exist.

So long as the bimetallic nation possesses
both gold and silver and is willing to exchange
them at 1 to $15\frac{1}{2}$, no other ratio can prevail.

CHAPTER XIII.

The currency of the world has never been settled by common consent. ALTHOUGH gold and silver have been used as money from the earliest period of which we have any record, the nations of the world have never combined to use them in the manner which would give the best results. Each nation has decided for itself whether it would use gold or silver, or both; and if it used both metals, it has decided from time to time at what ratio they should be a legal tender. Not unfrequently adjacent nations have had different ratios, with the inevitable result that each metal flowed towards the country in which the highest value was assigned to it. Very often the coinage has been debased, and sometimes Governments have taken possession of the mines and coined the produce according to their wishes at the time.

The result has been confusion. In matters of currency the nations of the world have been like men groping in the dark, and their perplexity cannot be better illustrated than by a consideration of the history of coinage in Great Britain, which will have the advantage of leading up to those changes inaugrated in 1871 which have led to the loss of the fixed-ratio between gold and silver.

The English standard was originally silver. The currency established in England by William the Conqueror was a purely silver currency, but in subsequent reigns the coins were frequently debased* by authority, and false coinage was habitual, notwithstanding the penalties of excommunication, and even of mutilation. In the reign of Edward III gold coins were for the first time made a legal tender, and the ratio of change between gold and silver coins was from time to time declared by the Government, an alteration being generally made when the silver coin was debased. In the time of James I it was found necessary to reduce the quantity of gold in the coins and to order that they should pass for a greater number of silver coins. This was done to prevent the gold coins from leaving the country. The change was effective for a time, and it actually become profitable to export silver instead of gold.

In the time of Charles II it was again found necessary to reduce the quantity of gold in the gold coins. Guineas were first coined in this reign, and were intended to pass current for 20 shillings ; but as this rate was not proclaimed by authority, the guinea actually circulated, by public consent, for 21 or 22 shillings, and the standard of the country again became silver monometallic.

In the reign of William III the silver coinage, which had become very much debased, was called in, and full coins issued at a cost to the nation of three millions sterling.

In 1717, on the advice of Sir Isaac Newton, the guinea was declared to be worth 21 shillings. The ratio thus established between silver

But the coinage was frequently debased.

And when gold was coined the ratio between gold and silver was frequently altered.

Under William III the purification of the coinage cost three millions sterling.

---

* An account of the debasement of the silver coin will be found in Lord Liverpool's Treatise on the Coins of the Realm. By nine successive debasements, beginning with Edward I and ending with Elizabeth, the Tower pound of sterling silver, which was at first coined into 20 shillings, came at last to be coined into 58s. 1¼d.

and gold was 1 to 15·21, and as in Spain, Holland, and other countries the ratio was 1 to 14 and 1 to 14·50, silver flowed out of England.

In 1730 the Spanish Government adopted the ratio of 1 to 15$\frac{7}{8}$, and then silver flowed back to England. In 1772 Spain reduced the quantity of gold in the gold coins so as to bring about a ratio of 1 to 16$\frac{1}{8}$. In 1774 the legal tender of silver coin in England was limited to £25, and it was declared that any offer of payment in silver in excess of £25 should only be a legal tender according to weight at the rate of 5s. 2d. for each ounce of silver. As the silver coin was generally below weight at the time, the practical effect of this law was to establish gold coin as the only full legal tender money, though silver was not formally deprived of its status of legal tender till a later period. The total coinage of silver at the mint from 1717 to 1800 did not much exceed half a million sterling, and a considerable portion of this silver had been taken in war.

In 1786 Spain altered the ratio to 1 to 16$\frac{1}{2}$. But the standard of England was practically gold, and continued to be so until 1797, when the Bank of England suspended cash payments, and Bank of England notes became practically a legal tender.

In 1816 England adopted a gold standard, and in 1821 the Bank of England resumed cash payments.

Adoption of the ratio of 1 to 15¼ by France.

In 1803 France adopted the legal ratio of 1 to 15$\frac{1}{2}$, and as the French metallic coinage was sufficiently large to maintain this ratio against other countries, it became the ratio of the civilised world, until, after the lapse of 70 years, France refused to coin silver freely, and so destroyed the ratio.

The effect of the legal French ratio of 1 to 15½ in steadying the price of silver up to 1870 is shown by the following table, which I have extracted from a work by Ernest Seyd :— Effect of the French ratio on the price of silver.

Years.	Percentage in value of gold production to silver production.	Relative value of gold and silver in Hamburgh from 1801 to 1832, and in London from 1832 to 1870.
1801—1810 ...	24 to 76	1 to 15·61
1811—1820 ...	25 to 75	1 to 15·51
1821—1830 ...	33 to 67	1 to 15·80
1831—1840 ...	35 to 65	1 to 15·75
1841—1850 ...	52 to 48	1 to 15·83
1851—1855 ...	78 to 22	1 to 15·76
1856—1860 ...	78 to 22	1 to 15·76
1861—1865 ...	74 to 26	1 to 15·48
1866—1870 ...	69 to 31	1 to 15·48

During the whole of the period to which this table refers France was never completely denuded of either silver or gold, and was always prepared to coin either gold or silver into legal tender money at the ratio of 1 to 15½. If, then, there is truth in the bimetallic theory, the ratio of gold to silver must have been maintained at 1 to 15½.

An examination of the last column of the table shows that the ratio in Hamburgh and London was maintained very nearly at 1 to 15½, but that there were slight variations, the ratio ranging between 1 to 15·48 and 1 to 15·83. The explanation of these slight variations is this :—The ratio of France was 1 to 15½ ; a merchant in London, who had gold for which he wished to get silver, was obliged, when silver was not forthcoming in London, to incur the costs of sending his gold to Paris ; he could then exchange it for silver at 1 to 15½ (paying, however, a trifling sum to induce the Banks to take Explanation of the slight variation in the market price of silver from the French legal ratio.

the trouble of giving him silver instead of gold), and he had also to bear the cost of bringing his silver back to London. In these circumstances the person who wished to exchange gold for silver in London would get something less than 15½ lbs. of silver for one lb. of gold when there was a flow of gold towards France. If it so happened that there was a flow of silver at the time towards France, he would get rather better terms than 15½ lbs. of silver for one lb. of gold, because the holders of silver could only get one lb. of gold for 16½ lbs. of silver after they had sent their silver to France, and they would consequently be prepared to sell their silver on easier terms in London and so save the cost of transport. Allowing for inevitable slight fluctuations due to these causes, we see that the French bimetallic system did absolutely maintain the ratio of 1 to 15½ between gold and silver down to 1870.

The steadiness in the price of silver from 1803 to 1870 conclusive as to the possibility of maintaining a fixed ratio between the values of gold and silver.

It has already been shown at page 8 that in the first half of the present century the value of the silver in the world exceeded the value of the gold, and that silver discharged a larger proportion of the duties of money than did gold, the ratio being about 8 to 5. In these circumstances, if the bimetallic theory be wrong, a constant market ratio could only have been preserved between silver and gold if the production of the two metals had been in the proportion of 8 to 5; in other words, if the production of each metal had been exactly proportioned to the extent to which it discharged the duties of money.

The relative production of silver and gold during the first 20 years of this period was very nearly as 8 to 2⅔, and yet a constant ratio between the two metals was maintained. During

a second period of 20 years the ratio of production was very nearly as 8 to 4, and the same
relative value of $15\frac{1}{2}$ to 1 was maintained.
From 1841 to 1850 the ratio of production was
nearly 8 to 8, and yet the ratio of value was
maintained at $15\frac{1}{2}$ to 1. From 1851 to 1860
the ratio of production was not far from 8 to
28, and yet the ratio of value was still maintained at $15\frac{1}{2}$ to 1. From 1861 to 1865 the
ratio of production did not vary greatly from
8 to 23, and from 1866 to 1870 it was 8 to 18,
and yet the ratio of value remained at $15\frac{1}{2}$ to 1.

To contend, in face of the facts seated in this
chapter, that the legal ratio fixed under the
bimetallic system between gold and silver when
used as money will not control and regulate the
market price of the two metals, is simply to
abandon reason, argument, and experience, and
take refuge in assertion.

CHAPTER XIV.

CAUSE OF THE DIVERGENCE IN THE RELATIVE
VALUE OF SILVER AND GOLD SINCE 1873.

The old ratio between gold and silver has ceased to exist. A RATIO of 1 to $15\frac{1}{2}$ between gold and silver corresponds to a price of $60\frac{7}{8}$d. per ounce for silver ; the present price of silver in London is about $47\frac{1}{2}$d. per ounce ; and the ratio of 1 to $15\frac{1}{2}$ between gold and silver, which was maintained from the beginning of the present century up to 1873, has ceased to exist. The relative production of silver and gold has been very nearly the same during the last few years. How then does it happen that the fixed relative value of gold and silver, which was maintained when the production of silver was three times that of gold, and again when the production of gold was nearly four times that of silver, has now completely disappeared ?

Demonetisation of silver by Germany. To answer this question we must go back to the Monetary Conference held at Paris in 1867. That Conference aimed at a universal uniform monetary unit to be established by international agreement, and, confining its attention to one aspect of the monetary question, recommended the universal adoption of the gold monometallic standard. Its recommendations bore no fruit for a time ; but when the King of Prussia became Emperor of Germany, and more intimate relations were established between the different German States, an obvious and valuable reform was the substitution of a currency issued under the authority of the German

Empire for the separate currencies of the different States. Germany possessed at this time the silver standard, and might under the new system have either continued that standard, or adopted the bimetallic standard ; but she had received an indemnity of £200,000,000 from France, and felt herself in a position to introduce the gold monometallic standard.

At this time some nations were gold monometallic, other silver monometallic, while others again were bimetallic. Several nations that were nominally monometallic with a gold or silver standard, and the United States that was nominally bimetallic at the rate of 1 to 16, possessed forced paper currencies. Many other nations had a gold, or silver, or a bimetallic standard, subject, however, to various defaults and limitations owing to restrictions placed by law on the coinage of one or other or both of these metals.

State of the currencies of the world in 1870.

The countries that effectively maintained the gold standard were Great Britain, Australia, the Cape, and Canada; the countries that maintained effectively the silver standard were China, India, Germany, Holland, Denmark, Sweden, Norway, and Mexico. The countries that really maintained the bimetallic system were France, Belgium, and Switzerland. The chief countries with a forced paper currency were Turkey and Brazil with a nominal gold standard, Italy and the United States with a nominal bimetallic standard (the latter at the non-effective rate of 1 to 16), and Austria and Russia with a nominal silver standard.

Germany took preliminary steps towards the demonetisation of silver in December 1871, brought the change into operation in July 1873, and no longer coins silver freely, although she has not been able to withdraw the whole of her silver money.

She was quickly followed by Denmark, Sweden, and Norway, who altered their silver standard to a gold standard in 1873. After 1874 Holland also ceased to coin silver as legal tender money, and in 1875 began to coin gold.

In 1874 the Latin Union—France, Belgium, Switzerland, and Italy—suspended the free coinage of silver, the bimetallic principle ceased to operate, and the ratio of exchange between gold and silver varied just as the ratio of exchange between any two commodities not used as money would vary.

As the effect of the changes initiated by Germany was to throw on the market a quantity of silver to be exchanged for gold, to limit the extent to which the duties of money were performed by silver, to increase the extent to which these duties were performed by gold, and as this change coincided with an increase in the production of silver as compared with gold, the inevitable result was a fall in the value of silver as compared with gold.

In 1873 America had altered her nominal bimetallic to a nominal gold standard. When she resumed specie payments, her nominal gold standard became a real standard, and an influence tending to raise gold still higher as compared with silver was brought into play, which has, however, been somewhat checked in its operation by the Bland Bill.

Under this law, passed in 1878, the United States must coin not less than 2,000,000 of dollars in silver every month at the ratio of 1 to 16, and has been doing so since 1878.

The total amount of silver coin coined under the Bland Bill up to 1st October 1884, was no less than 182,380,829 dollars. Against 96,491,251 dollars of this amount silver certificates has been issued, while 40,322,042 dollars had actually been put in circulation, and 45,567,536 dollars were lying idle in the treasury.

Of the silver dollars coined by America about one-fourth are lying idle.

The following table shows the average price of silver in London for every year since 1852:—

Fall in the price of silver since 1873.

	Per ounce. d.		Per ounce. d.
1852	$60\frac{11}{16}$	1869	$60\frac{1}{2}$
1853	$61\frac{1}{8}$	1870	$60\frac{1}{2}$
1854	$61\frac{1}{4}$	1871	$60\frac{9}{16}$
1855	$61\frac{1}{4}$	1872	$60\frac{1}{4}$
1856	$61\frac{7}{16}$	1873	$59\frac{1}{4}$
1857	$61\frac{3}{4}$	1874	$58\frac{5}{16}$
1858	$61\frac{7}{16}$	1875	$56\frac{3}{4}$
1859	$62\frac{1}{16}$	1876	$52\frac{3}{4}$
1860	$60\frac{11}{16}$	1877	$54\frac{13}{16}$
1861	$61\frac{3}{4}$	1878	$52\frac{9}{16}$
1862	$61\frac{3}{8}$	1879	$51\frac{1}{4}$
1863	$61\frac{1}{4}$	1880	$52\frac{1}{4}$
1864	$61\frac{3}{8}$	1881	$51\frac{11}{16}$
1865	61	1882	$51\frac{5}{8}$
1866	$61\frac{1}{8}$	1883	$50\frac{1}{16}$
1867	$60\frac{9}{16}$	1884	$50\frac{3}{4}$
1868	$60\frac{1}{2}$	1885 (to 20th October)	$48\frac{3}{8}$

CHAPTER XV.

EFFECTS OF THE DIVERGENCE IN THE VALUE
OF GOLD AND SILVER.

Silver fallen in value more than 19 per cent. as compared with gold. WE now come to the important question of the effects produced by the divergence in the relative value of silver and gold which has followed the legislation initiated in 1871.

Silver had fallen in value as compared with gold nearly 19 per cent. in the early part of 1885, and has since fallen even lower.

Burden imposed on all persons whose incomes are in silver and their expenditure in gold. The result of this fall, which causes the most frequent complaints, is the burden imposed thereby on all persons whose incomes are in silver and their expenditure in gold. Great hardship has been caused to all European officials serving in India, and the financial position of the Government of India has been seriously affected. The Government of India has large gold liabilities in England, and finds that these liabilities require for their discharge the payment of a very much larger number of rupees than was formerly the case.

Uncertainty introduced into certain classes of commercial transactions. Another evil is the additional uncertainty in the operations of commerce between gold-using and silver-using countries, due to the fluctuation in the relative value of gold and silver.

Obstruction to the free investment of capital. A further evil is the disinclination of capitalists to seek investments in countries that have a silver standard. The greatest reservoir of capital is to be found in London, and capitalists whose capital is in gold hesitate to invest their money in a country which has a silver coinage. A man who invested £1,000 sterling in India some years ago now finds that it is worth about £800, owing to the fall in the relative value of silver. Consequently capital is discouraged from flowing to silver countries. India looses because she has to pay a higher price for the capital she requires, and capitalists loose because India will not at this high rate take as much capital as she otherwise would. The evil is no imaginary one. The Government of India can borrow in gold nearly $\frac{3}{4}$ per cent. cheaper than it can borrow in silver. The Indian gold $3\frac{1}{2}$ per cent. stock is above par. The Indian silver 4 per cent. promissory notes are below par. The difficulties connected with the finding of capital for Indian Railways and for the great works projected by the Municipalities and Port Trusts of Bombay and Calcutta in the present day are of a very practical nature.

Although the evils just mentioned are of such magnitude that it would be very desirable to adopt measures for removing them, if this could be done otherwise than at an excessive cost, they are not intolerable, nor very grievous, except to the Indian Government and the limited number of people whose incomes are in silver and their expenditure, or a portion of it, in gold.

The question of the appreciation of gold *Appreciation* since the partial demonetisation of silver is of *of gold.* much more importance as regards the welfare and industry of the world.

The European nations have for the time practically demonetised silver, though they have refrained from throwing, except to a comparatively limited extent, their stock of silver on the public market.

Gold is now called on to do more work than it would have done if the old order of things had not been changed; to exactly the same extent silver is doing less work than it would have done. As gold is doing more work, the effect of the change must have tended to lower gold prices; as silver is doing less work, the effect of the change must have tended to raise silver prices.

The value of the total amount of gold in the hands of man is very nearly the same as the value of the total amount of silver: if France had remained bimetallic, the amount of work done by gold and silver respectively would have been automatically adjusted so as to preserve the ratio of 1 to $15\frac{1}{2}$; as matters now stand gold does more work than it would have done, and silver does less work by exactly the same amount; the extent to which prices have been lowered in the case of gold should, therefore, be very nearly the same as the extent to which they have been raised in the case of silver.

The most probable hypothesis is that gold prices have been lowered 9·5 per cent. and silver prices raised by the same amount.

The total divergence between gold and silver being taken at 19 per cent., we might fairly expect that the changes made since 1871 should have lowered gold prices about 9·5 per cent., and should have raised silver prices by about the same percentage.

And here I would caution the reader that it does not necessarily follow from what has been said above that gold prices must have actually fallen or silver prices risen, or that gold prices must have fallen as much as 9·5 per cent., or silver prices risen in a like proportion. The influences which affect prices are infinite in number and variety. The quantity of gold or

silver used as money is only one of these influences, and the effect of the appreciation of
gold, or depreciation of silver, may be aggravated, or counteracted, or entirely obscured, by
an increase or decrease of production, by the
extension or restriction of credit, as well as by
many other causes. We cannot say that the
more extended use of gold has actually lowered gold prices by 9·5 per cent., or that the
limitation of the area within which silver is
used has actually raised silver prices by 9·5 per
cent.

But the effect
on prices of the
relative rise of
gold and fall
of silver in
value may be
obscured by
many other in-
fluences.

All we can say is that gold prices would in
all probability be 9·5 per cent. higher than they
actually are if there had been no change in the
relative use of gold and silver, and that silver
prices would in the same case have probably
been lower by 9·5 per cent.

It will also of course be understood that I do
not for a moment mean to say that the tendency
to higher or lower prices is to be measured by
the exact percentage of 9·5 in each case. The
total divergence between gold and silver is
about 19 per cent.; and the most probable
supposition we can make is that half of the
divergence is due to appreciation of gold, and
half to depreciation of silver. But the appreciation of gold may have been more, and the
depreciation of silver less, or the opposite. All
we know with certainty is that the appreciation
of gold *plus* the depreciation of silver, due to
the partial demonetisation of silver, has amount-
ed to a variation of 19 per cent.; and it will be
obvious that wherever the same commodities are
bought and sold for gold and silver, a variation
of 19 per cent. in the relative value of gold and
silver must be followed by a variation of exactly

In any market
where gold,
silver, and
commodities
generally are
exchanged
against each
other, the
change in the
relative value
of gold and
silver must
have produced
a variation of
equal amount
in gold and sil-
ver prices.

the same amount between the gold and silver prices of commodities.

Whether the effect has been to make gold prices lower than they would otherwise have been by 19 per cent. or silver prices higher by 19 per cent., or whether gold prices have been kept down to the extent of 9·5 per cent. and silver prices kept higher by 9·5 per cent., we cannot say ; but the last supposition is certainly the more probable.

The evidence of an actual fall in gold prices in recent years is overwhelming, and will be considered in a separate chapter.

CHAPTER XVI.

THE FALL IN GOLD PRICES.

In examining the question of the fall in gold prices it will be best to go back for a number of years to inquire what has been the actual course of prices during the past half century, to note the causes which have produced fluctuation, and then to endeavour to ascertain to what extent prices have fallen since the partial demonetisation of silver.

The first authority to whom I shall appeal is the late Mr. William Newmarch. *Opinion of Mr. Newmarch.*

In May 1878 Mr. Newmarch read a paper before the Statistical Society "On the Progress of the Foreign Trade of the United Kingdom from 1856 to 1877," in which he made some valuable remarks on the course of gold prices.

When the great gold discoveries took place in the middle of the present century, Mr. Newmarch was one of the few persons who held that the extravagant anticipations of rise in prices, owing to the increased supply of gold, held by most persons, were erroneous, "and that after a short time the extension of commerce, the stimulus given to invention and enterprise by fresh markets, and the consequent infinite multiplication of transactions far exceeding any previous experience, would prevent before long any undue rise of prices by mere force of increased quantity on the side of the new gold ; that most emphatically the end to be feared was, not that the new supplies of gold would continue, but that by any possibility they might fall away or cease; and, in short, that the world ought to rejoice if a new gold-field could be discovered every few years."

In dealing with the subject of prices, Mr. Newmarch made use of the average price, mostly in London, of the chief commodities of raw materials, food, and tropical produce, and carried his inquiries, with the help of figures given by Professor Jevons, back to the year 1831.

Fall in prices in the period immediately preceding the great gold discoveries of the present century.

The following table shows the progress of prices, according to Mr. Newmarch, from 1831 to 1850, the period immediately preceding the great gold discoveries :—

All commodities observed.	Average price.
1831—35	114
1836—40	124
1841—45	107
1846—50	100

These figures indicate a marked fall in prices during the 20 years ending with 1850.

On this point Mr. Newmarch remarks as follows :—

"Careful observers had begun to recognise the fact, of which there is now no question, viz., that for about 20 years prior to 1848 the annual supplies of gold had been insufficient to meet the wear and tear of the coin in use, the requirements of the arts, and the needs of enlarging industry, commerce, and population. There had been a slow, but steady and progressive, tendency towards lower prices; and, therefore, towards a discouragement of enterprise in which lapse of time and the state of distant markets had to be considered."

Before 1847 the annual supply of gold had been about 4 millions sterling yearly. In 1850 it rose to 9 millions sterling, and in 1856 it is believed to have exceeded 32 millions sterling. From that date there has been a steady tendency to decrease, and in the present day the total production is believed to be under 20 millions sterling.

The effect on prices of the increased production of gold was very marked, as the following table, taken from Mr. Newmarch, shows :— *Rise of prices after the great gold discoveries.*

All commodities observed.	Average price.
Average of 1851 and 1853 ...	112
Average from 1857 to 1859 ...	125
Average from 1860 to 1864 ...	141
Average from 1865 to 1869 ...	138
Average from 1870 to 1874 ...	128
Average from 1875 to 1877 ...	125

The American War affected the average from 1860 to 1869 by raising the price of cotton and other articles, but, making every allowance for this influence, we see that the gold discoveries of the middle of the century were followed by a rise of prices, which showed signs of falling off after 1869, though no very marked change could be traced even in the period extending from 1870 to 1877.

In January 1879 Mr. Robert Giffen read a paper before the Statistical Society in which he dealt with the question of the fall of prices of commodities. *Opinion of Mr. Giffen.*

He took sixteen commodities which had been selected in 1874 as being fairly representative and suitable for recording prices, and he showed that between 1st January 1873 and 1st January 1879 there had been a fall of price varying *Serious fall in prices between 1873 and 1879.*

from 66 to 10 per cent. in the case of different articles.

To obviate the objection that he was comparing a period of depression with one of inflation, he examined prices for a series of years, and came to the conclusion that there was a great unusual fall. He ascribed the fall to a great stimulus to production, to the bad harvests of 1875, 1876, and 1877, and to the appreciation of gold.

Fall in prices held by Mr. Giffen to be partly due to insufficiency of supply of gold to meet the demands on it. The appreciation of gold he held to be due to the extraordinary demands upon it to supply Germany with a new gold coinage and to enable the United States to resume specie payments.

But he was not disposed to ascribe the whole of the fall in prices to the temporary and extraordinary demands of Germany and the United States. I quote his own words :—

" The question is infallibly suggested, however, whether there is not a subtler cause at work—an actual insufficiency of the current supply of gold for the current demands of gold-using countries."

His opinion in 1879 was that some such cause probably was at work, and he based this conclusion on the undoubted falling off of gold supplies during the preceding 20 years, coupled with the " enormous increase of current demands."

These current demands were due to increase of population, wealth, and trade, as well as to an extension of the area of gold-using countries by the inclusion of France, Germany, and the United States.

" In this view the fall of prices in the last ten years has been aggravated by a subtler cause than the extraordinary demands for gold which have existed. These demands have come upon a market which apparently had no surplus to spare. They have consequently been supplied very largely by a continued pressure upon existing stocks, till an adjustment has at length been made by a contraction of trade and a fall in values."

Mr. Giffen evidently anticipated in 1879 a further fall in prices from the continued scarcity of gold, and though he did not look with the same apprehension on the result that many other authorities expressed, the practical conclusion he drew was—" That the scarcity of gold which has contributed to the present fall of prices, and may have further serious effects in future, should, if possible, be mitigated, and should at any rate not be aggravated, by legislative action." He declared against the abolition of small notes by countries which still retained them, on the ground that it would lead to a further demand for the precious metal, and added :—" Still more we ought to deprecate any change in silver-using countries in the direction of substituting gold for any part of the silver in use. It would be nothing short of calamitous to business if another demand for gold like the recent demands from Germany and the United States were now to spring up."

Mr. Giffen opposed to any further demonetisation of silver.

CHAPTER XVII.

Opinion of Mr.
Goschen that
the fall in gold
prices is due to
the additional
burden thrown
on gold.

In April 1883 the Right Hon' Mr. Goschen, M.P., read a paper before the Institute of Bankers on the " Probable Results of an Increase in the Purchasing Power of Gold," in which he carried somewhat further the line of argument adopted by Mr. Giffen.

Mr. Goschen estimated that in the 10 years ending 1883 no less than £200,000,000 sterling had been required for the purpose of providing a new gold coinage for Germany, Italy, and the United States of America.

He held that the application of £200,000,000 of gold to purposes for which it had not been required 10 or 14 years before must, *cæteris paribus*, cause a fall in prices ; and he brought forward tables showing that there had been a remarkable fall between 1873 and 1883.

The following table was given by him to illustrate this portion of the question :—

Commodity	Prices in 1873 (£ s d)	Prices in 1883 (£ s d)
Sugar—Brown Manilla …	0 16 6 per cwt.	0 5 0 to 0 12 0 per cwt.
Good and fine West Indian …	1 9 0 "	1 0 0 "
Tea—sound common Congou …	0 0 11½ per lb.	0 0 5¼ per lb.
Coffee—Middling Plantation Ceylon …	4 7 0 per cwt.	3 10 0 per cwt.
Cocoa—Guayaquil …	3 19 0 to 3 0 0 "	2 19 0 "
Wheat …	2 16 0 per qr.	2 0 6 per qr.
Rice—Rangoon …	0 9 6 per cwt.	0 7 0 per cwt.
Pepper …	0 0 7 per lb.	0 0 5¼ per lb.
Iron—Scotch pig …	6 7 0 per ton.	2 9 0 per ton.
Lead—English …	21 10 0 "	13 15 0 "
Copper …	91 0 0 "	65 0 0 "
Tin—Foreign … *	142 0 0 "	93 0 0 "
Wool—English Sheep's, half Hog, half Wether …	0 2 3 per lb.	0 0 10¾ per lb.
Mohair …	0 3 3 "	0 1 8¼ "
Australian—Average Victoria Washed …	0 2 9 "	0 1 10 "
Alpaca …	0 0 9 "	0 1 3 "
Cotton—Middling Upland …	0 0 6¼ "	0 0 5½ "
Fair Surat …	0 2 5 "	0 0 4¼ "
Cochineal …	0 7 6 "	0 10 0 "
Indigo …	0 7 3 to 0 8 0 "	0 6 6 to 0 6 10 "
Hides—River Plate, heavy salted …	0 0 8½ "	0 0 7¼ "
Light …	0 0 8¼ "	0 0 6½ "
Jute …	16 0 0 per ton.	10 10 0 to 11 0 0 per ton.
Nitrate of Soda …	0 16 0 to 0 16 6 per cwt.	0 12 0 per cwt.
Saltpetre …	1 10 6 "	0 19 0 "
Coals, Wallsend …	1 10 0 per ton.	0 18 0 per ton.

Mr. Goschen also gave a table showing the prices of certain other articles in 1873 and 1881 :—

	1873.			1881.		
	£	*s*	*d*	£	*s*	*d*
Paper for writing and printing...	3	0	9	1	16	3
Silk, per lb.	1	1	0	0	17	0
Timber, per load, hewn ...	3	5	0	2	12	0
Stones	10	0	0	5	0	0
Mahogany	11	12	0	9	5	0
Railway carriages	111	10	0	85	0	0
Boots and Shoes, per doz. pairs...	3	4	9	2	17	2

The fall in price shown by these tables proves that the purchasing power of gold increased in a very remarkable degree after 1873.

The year 1873 one of inflation.

It was contended, in opposition to Mr. Goschen's view, that a comparison of the prices of 1883 with that of 1873 was not a fair comparison, because 1873 was a year of inflation, when prices were specially high. This objection is not without force, as will be seen by an examination of the figures given by Mr. Newmarch.

Mr. Newmarch's figures for the period from 1865 to 1877 are as follow :—

1865	...	...	...	152
1866	...	...	...	150
1867	...	...	...	133
1868	...	...	...	129
1869	...	...	...	123
1870	...	...	...	121
1871	...	...	...	120
1872	...	...	...	135
1873	...	...	...	135
1874	...	...	...	130
1875	...	...	...	125
1876	...	...	...	120
1877	...	...	...	121

These figures show that 1872 and 1873 were years of high prices as compared with the four preceding years.

But even after making every allowance for the high prices of 1873, a very remarkable fall of prices during the last ten years or so has taken place. This was shown by Mr. Goschen in a letter to the *Times*, in which he appealed to so-called " index numbers " given every year by the *Economist*, which represent the wholesale prices of twenty-two of the most important commodities of the English market in successive years, and which may be taken as an approximate measure of the rise or fall in prices.

The figures of the *Economist* are here given :—

Year.		Total Index No.
1845—50	... ...	2,200
1857, July 1st	... ...	2,996
1858, January	... ...	2,612
1866 ,,	... ...	3,564
1867 ,,	... ...	3,024
1870 ,,	... ...	2,689
1871 ,,	... ...	2,590
1872 ,,	.. ...	2,835
1873 ,,	... ...	2,947
1874 ,,	... ...	2,891
1875 ,,	... ...	2,778
1876 ,,	... ...	2,711
1877 ,,	... ...	2,723
1878 ,,	... ...	2,529
1879 ,,	... ...	2,202
1880 ,,	... ...	2,538
1881 ,,	... ...	2,376
1882 ,,	... ...	2,435
1883 ,,	... ...	2,343
1884 ,,	... ...	2,221*
1885 ,,	... ...	2,098*

This table is conclusive as to the great fall in prices which has taken place of late years— a fall which is remarkably steady in its nature, and which has now brought prices back to the old level of 1845—50 before the great gold discoveries. There is, indeed, no room for

But, apart from the inflation of 1873, there has been a continuous and steady fall in prices.

---

* These figures are taken from an article by Mr. Giffen published in the *Contemporary Review* for June 1885.

argument on this point; and the only question is to what extent the fall in price is due to the greater demand for gold in consequence of the partial demonetisation of silver and of the substitution of gold for paper in Italy and America.

Opinion of Mr. Hansard that the fall in prices was due mainly to cheaper production and over supply.

This aspect of the question was dealt with by Mr. Hansard in a paper read before the Institute of Bankers in December 1884. Mr. Hansard examined the prices of twenty-five commodities during the years from 1874 to 1883 inclusive. He found that the prices of twenty-one commodities had fallen as compared with 1874, while during the same period the stock in hand of fifteen articles had increased and the stock in hand of ten had decreased.

Of the ten commodities showing a decrease in stock, seven also showed a decrease in price. Mr. Hansard gave reasons for supposing that the effective stock was really greater than his figures showed in the case of articles which apparently had not increased in stock. But all speculations of this kind are uncertain, and the reverse process might be applied to all commodities which had apparently increased in stock.

Mr. Hansard's final conclusions were that there had been a marked and general fall in prices during the decade 1874—83; that the fall had occurred, partly owing to greater facilities of production, and consequent lessened cost, than formerly, but mainly from over-production; and that this over-production had probably been caused by the opening up of new and more abundant sources of supply.

Opinion of M. Paul Leroy-Beaulieu.

M. Paul Leroy-Beaulieu appears to take the same view as Mr. Hansard, witness the following passage written in April 1884 :—

" It is evident then that there can be no
doubt of the actual existence of this diminution of prices, and on this point one can hardly
understand that there should be any diversity
of opinion. We ourselves had found during
the last two years that prices had become, if
not universally, yet generally, lower, and the
decline moreover has been for the most part of
a permanent and durable character, and not
merely a temporary fluctuation, which will be
corrected by an immediate rebound.

" It is even more than probable that as regards a vast number of articles this decline will
eventually become more accentuated ; and we
must express our firm conviction that the period is not far remote when the prices of the
greater part of the necessaries of life will be
within the reach of all at a considerably reduced rate.

" To account for this decline there are many
circumstances which must be taken into consideration ; but the causes which have been
chiefly instrumental in producing it may be
summed up as follow :—the opening up and
development of new countries, or the regenera-
tion of old ones which had fallen into barbarism
and have been reclaimed and brought under the
influence of civilisation ; the increased facilities
in the means of transport, and the state of per-
fection to which they have been brought, and
the continual reductions which are being made
in tariffs and tolls on railways and canals ; the
constant augmentation of capital and increase
of industrial competition, both of which are instrumental in causing the rate of interest to be
lowered, and in forcing the trading community
to be content with very moderate profits."

Fall in prices probably due to several causes.

It must be admitted that the arguments of Mr. Hansard and M. Paul Leroy-Beaulieu have much force in them, and that the causes stated by them have had a great, and no doubt a lasting, influence on prices. But, on the other hand, I find it equally impossible to believe that the monetary legislation initiated in 1871, which has caused so great a divergence in the value of gold and silver during the last 12 years, has not also had a very material influence on prices.

Formerly gold and silver divided the duty of money between them in such manner as to preserve a constant ratio of value of 1 to $15\frac{1}{2}$.

Now the duty discharged by gold has been increased, and that discharged by silver diminished, so that latterly the ratio has varied between 1 to 19 and 1 to 20.

This change must have either tended to cause gold prices to fall or silver prices to rise, or must have had both effects. What grounds have we for saying that it has not affected gold prices, but has affected silver prices ? Would it not be just as reasonable to say that it has not affected silver prices, but has affected gold prices ? And is it not certain that it has acted partly in the one direction and partly in the other ?

Increased supply of commodities has no doubt affected prices, but I do not see why we should doubt that the increased demand for gold has also affected them. Two causes are shown to exist which would tend to lower prices, and it would be unreasonable to say that the actual fall in prices is due to one only of these causes.

There certainly has been of late years a remarkable correspondence between the range of prices in England and the rate of exchange between gold and silver. I place side by side the index numbers of the *Economist* for every year since 1873, and also the price of silver per ounce on the corresponding date—

Year.	Index No.	Prices of silver per oz.
1873	2947	59¾
1874	2891	59
1875	2778	57¾
1876	2711	55½
1877	2723	57¼
1878	2529	53½
1879	2202	49⅞
1880	2538	52 1/16
1881	2376	51
1882	2435	52
1883	2343	50 1/16
1884	2221	51
1885	2098	49¼

The coincidence shown in this table cannot be the result of accident.

Prices are high in England when exchange with the silver-using countries is high, and *vice versâ*. But it cannot fairly be said that it is the low rate of exchange that makes low prices, because low prices in England have also the effect of reducing the rate of exchange. When the price of silver falls, there is a tendency to a fall of gold prices of commodities in England; when the gold prices of commodities fall, there is a tendency to a lower price for silver.

The two causes react on each other, and in the present day the rate of exchange in India and the general prices of commodities in England rise and fall together.

I see no reason to doubt that a bimetallic system with a fixed ratio between gold and silver would have a steadying influence on prices in England, and would tend to keep them at a higher level.

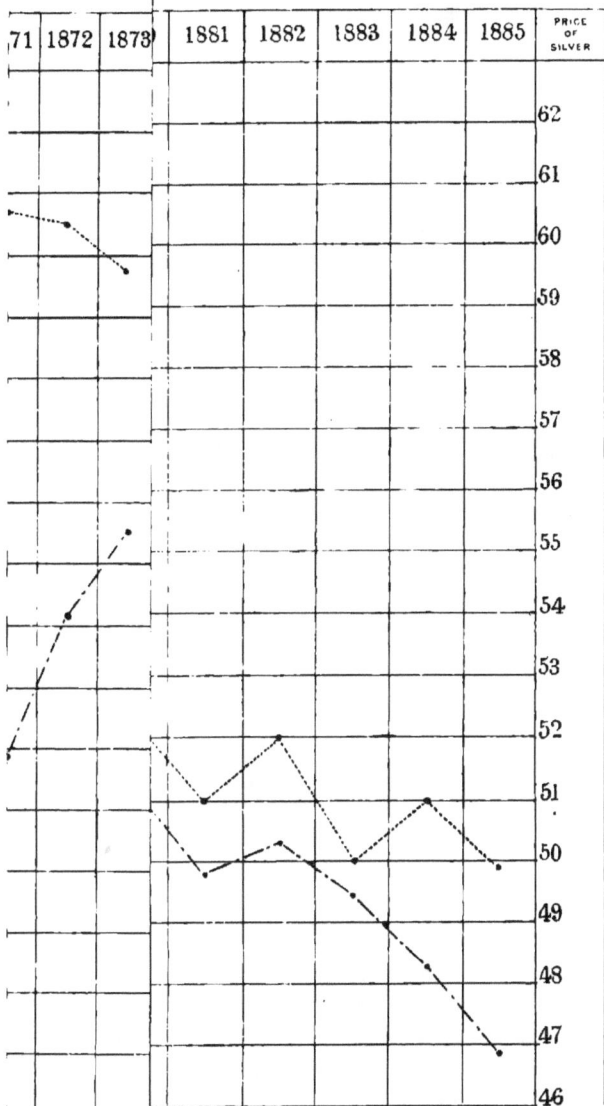

71	1872	1873	1881	1882	1883	1884	1885	PRICE OF SILVER

rice of silver, ng to the Index Nos. of the *Economist*, and

he line — - — - — the Index Nos.

ve been very great.

modities in England rise and fall together.

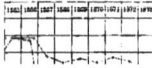

1985	1986	1987	1988	1989	1970	1971	1972	1973

CHAPTER XVIII.

RATIO OF EXCHANGE OF COMMODITIES FOR SILVER
IN ENGLAND SINCE 1845, AND LATEST OPINION
OF MR. GIFFEN.

To ascertain what has been the exchange value of commodities in comparison with silver in the English market, I have converted the index numbers of the *Economist* into figures which represent silver prices, according to the price of silver on the dates to which the numbers refer. The result is given in the following table, in which I have also given the average of the gold and silver prices; these average prices may, for the sake of argument, be assumed to represent both gold and silver prices, as they would have stood if France had not stopped the free coinage of silver at the old fixed ratio.

Silver prices of commodities in the English market.

In preparing the table on p. 76 I have taken the price of silver from 1845 to 1850 as the standard, and consequently the gold index number for that period is the same as the silver index number. From 1857 to 1874 the gold and silver index numbers closely agree, because the French bimetallic ratio prevailed during that period, and the market price of silver could only vary slightly from that ratio; the silver index numbers are, however, rather lower than the gold numbers, because from 1857 to 1874 the price of silver was rather higher than it was during 1845—50.

Year.	Total Index No. (gold.)	Total Index No. (silver.)	Average.
1845—60	2200	2200	2200
1857, July 1st ...	2996	2892	2944
1858, January 1st ...	2612	2529	2570
1865 ,, ...	3575	3458	3517
1866 ,, ...	3564	3437	3501
1867 ,, ...	3024	2958	2991
1868 ,, ...	2682	2635	2659
1869 ,, ...	2666	2613	2640
1870 ,, ...	2689	2641	2665
1871 ,, ...	2590	2547	2568
1872 ,, ...	2835	2790	2812
1873 ,, ...	2947	2933	2940
1874 ,, ...	2891	2930	2911
1875 ,, ...	2778	2874	2826
1876 ,, ...	2711	2905	2808
1877 ,, ...	2723	2832	2777
1878 ,, ..	2529	2791	2660
1879 ,, ..	2202	2642	2422
1880 ,, ..	2538	2889	2714
1881 ,, ...	2376	2774	2575
1882 ,, ...	2435	2787	2611
1883 ,, ...	2343	2786	2565
1884 ,, ...	2221	2593	2407
1885 ,, ...	2098	2505	2302

Since the partial demonetisation of silver, both gold and silver prices have fallen, but the former fell more rapidly and to a lower point.

After 1873 gold prices gradually declined, and so did silver prices, but the latter fell more slowly than the former, and, with the exception of 1879, showed no serious decline till 1884. After 1877 the fall in gold prices was very rapid, and has been practically continuous up to the present year.

If the bimetallic ratio had been maintained, we know that prices, both gold and silver, would have lain somewhere between what has been the actual course of gold prices and of silver prices ; would, in fact, have taken some such course as that indicated by the arithmetical mean between the two sets of prices.

We see then, that notwithstanding the relative depreciation of silver consequent on the monetary changes begun in 1871, the high prices of 1872 and 1873 have not been maintained in silver. The partial demonetisation of silver has not caused a rise in silver prices, but appears to have checked the fall which would otherwise have taken place. Even in silver prices the fall has been very great in 1884 and 1885.

The partial demonetisation checked the fall in silver prices, which would in any case have occurred.

The most probable conclusion is that, even if silver had not been partially demonetised in Europe, gold prices would have fallen, but that they would neither have fallen so rapidly nor so far as they have done.

And aggravated the inevitable fall in gold prices.

I cannot doubt that both parties have right on their side in their controversy as to the cause in the fall of gold prices—that gold prices have fallen on account of the increased supply of commodities, and that they have also fallen on account of the increased share of the duty of money thrown on gold. The values in silver of the principal commodities of the English market fell very little before 1884. In 1884 and 1885 the fall in silver prices also has been marked. The obvious conclusion is that the increased supply of silver in proportion to the share of work it had to do has partially counteracted a fall in silver prices that would otherwise have taken place. In any case there would have been a fall in prices ; the fall in gold prices has been aggravated by the partial demonetisation of silver ; the fall in silver prices has been mitigated by the same cause.

The question of the fall in prices was again discussed by Mr. Giffen in an article published in the *Contemporary Review* for June 1885.

Latest opinion of Mr. Giffen.

His conclusion is that, "Taking a still more extended view of the subject, there seems no small reason to believe that, whatever may be the cause, the course of prices in the wholesale markets has of late years taken a decided turn. There is at least some evidence that, for fifteen or twenty years after 1845—50, prices on the average tended to rise from period to period ; from about 1860 to 1873 they were comparatively stationary, oscillating between the highest maxima and minima which had come to be established ; and since 1873 the tendency has been downward, the oscillations now being much the same as before 1850, if not at a lower level." Mr. Giffen supports his conclusion as to a fall of prices by a reference to the index numbers of the *Economist*, which have already been given at page 73, and need not be here repeated.

Evidence of the index number of English Imports and Exports. He also refers to the index numbers contained in the Parliamentary Reports on the prices of Imports and Exports, and shows that the prices of exports have not been so low since 1840 as they are at the present time.

Taking 65·8 as his *datum* for exports, he informs us that this number falls to be increased or diminished in the years since 1840 as follows :—

Year.		Increase.		Decrease.
1840	...	13·34	...	—
1841	...	10·95	...	—
1845	...	6·05	...	—
1848	...	—	...	2·43
1849	...	—	...	5·29
1852	...	—	...	6·47
1853	...	—	...	1·14
1854	...	—	...	0·95
1855	...	—	...	2·75
1857	...	0·77	...	—
1859	...	0·40	...	—
1865	...	23·46	...	—
1868	...	11·42	...	—
1873	...	19·93	...	—

Year.	Increase.	Decrease.
1875	... 8 67	... —
1876	... 2·25	... —
1877	... —	... 0·40
1879	... —	... 6·10
1881	... —	... 6·26
1883	... —	... 5·95

Similarly, Mr. Giffen states that, as regards imports, the index number of 81·16 falls to be increased or diminished as follows :—

Year.	Increase.	Decrease.
1854	... —	... 0 80
1855	... 3·51	... —
1857	... 7·08	... —
1859	... —	... 1·39
1865	... 13·59	... —
1868	... 5·73	... —
1873	... 4·43	... —
1875	... 0·25	... —
1876	... —	... 3·61
1877	... —	... 1·48
1878	... —	... 7·04
1879	... —	... 10·30
1880	... —	... 6·39
1881	... —	... 6·99
1884	... —	... 9·43

With reference to these tables, Mr. Giffen adds : " The evidence is thus cumulative as to what the course of prices has been since 1850, and as to the general course having been very different since 1860—73 from what it was before. Not only do the index numbers prepared by Mr. Newmarch many years ago, and without any possible foresight of existing controversies, support this view, but index numbers based entirely on the actual proportions to each other of the different articles of our foreign trade bear testimony to the same fact. It is impossible to suppose that any other index numbers which could be impartially constructed would yield any other result. Every important article of commerce is included in them, and the oscillations of prices they respectively indicate synchronise in a striking manner."

Of the causes affecting prices Mr. Giffen attaches the greater weight to the insufficiency of the gold supply.

The fall in prices is beyond question, and in all probability it is a permanent fall, and very possibly a fall of which we have as yet by no means seen the end. Mr. Giffen mentions the two causes that have been suggested—one a great multiplication of commodities and diminution of the cost of production, the other a diminished production of gold and increased demand for it. To the latter of these causes he attaches the greater weight.

Finally, Mr. Giffen remarks: " There has been no marked increase in the rates of wages since 1873, and there are now in the directions reports of strikes and lower wages ; rents are undoubtedly falling; the income tax assessments have increased more languidly since 1875 than they did for many years before ; the returns of property liable to legacy and succession duty, though these are most difficult to fall owing to the naturally great fluctuations, would also appear of late years to have been stationary or declining. The very things are happening which we should have expected to happen if there had been a pressure upon gold."

Mr. Giffen anticipates a progressive and gradual fall in prices.

Mr. Giffen looks forward to a progressive but gradual fall in prices, but he does not view this result with apprehension. Trade will be sounder and industry steadier under a *régime* of steadily falling prices, and it would be as well to let things alone. Above all he holds

He holds bimetallism would be wholly inapplicable as a cure.

that the schemes of bimetallists would be wholly inapplicable as a cure for the evils to be apprehended. Assuming these schemes to be successful, " the future course of prices would be regulated by the aggregate annual production, not of the one metal, but of the two. The proportion of that annual production to the stocks of the two in use is, however, much the same as the production of the one metal to the stock of that metal only. The future course of prices will accordingly be much the same as if one metal only were used. The multiplication of commodities out of all proportion to the increased means of production of the precious metals will go on, and falling prices will inevitably result."

To those who have read Chapters V and VI of the present work, it will, perhaps, be unnecessary to use arguments in this place in opposition to Mr. Giffen's conclusion regarding the inapplicability of bimetallism as a panacea for existing evils. Nobody but a fanatic would hold that the adoption of bimetallism would instantly create wealth, remove all commercial difficulties, and make everybody prosperous for all time. But if a system of currency will remove or mitigate some of the evils from which we now suffer, will obviate dangers with which we are threatened in the future, and will bring no evils of its own in its train, it is not reasonable to reject it on the ground that it will not remove every evil and smooth away all difficulties. Even if it be accepted that there will probably be a progressive fall in prices, it would be better for the world that the fall should be gradual rather than abrupt. Although the production of gold and silver bears about the same proportion respectively to the actual stocks of these metals in the present day, this has not been the case in the past, and probably will not be so in the future ; two metals used as a fixed ratio must give more even prices than two metals used independently in different coun-

Bimetallism would not remove all evils

But it would remove some.

And would alleviate others.

tries; and, so long as the metals are not linked by a fixed ratio, we have no guarantee that extraordinary demands will not fall on one of them such as fell on gold by the action of Germany, the United States, and Italy; finally our inability to avert the effects of a calamity is is no reason why we should not mitigate them to the extent which is within our means. The equanimity with which Mr. Giffen contemplates a progressive fall in prices would not, if we are to judge from the passage quoted at page 62, have been shared by the late Mr. Newmarch. "Most emphatically the end to be feared was, not that the new supplies of gold would continue, but that by all possibility they might fall away or cease; and, in short, that the world ought to rejoice if a new gold field could be discovered every few years."

And would obviate the risk of future disaster.

Large supplies of gold are required every year to meet the increasing volume of commerce, while the actual yield of the mines has fallen away, and the stock of gold in the world has been subjected to extraordinary demands, and yet we are told that it would be futile to take such steps as are within our power to remove from gold the further and increasing burden imposed upon it by the partial demonetisation of silver, and to obviate the risks to which we are exposed in the future.

CHAPTER XIX.

It has already been shown that since the
partial demonetisation of silver in Europe gold
prices have fallen steadily and largely, and that
this fall is attributed by one school to appreciation of gold due to the larger demands made
upon it, and by the other to the increased production (using the words in their widest sense)
of commodities.

Any examination of the silver question
would be incomplete which left out of sight
the effects produced in those countries which
retained the silver standard. The chief of
those countries is India, and to it I propose to
confine my remarks.

When silver first fell largely in value as
compared with gold, many English economists,
and among them the late Mr. Walter Bagehot,
declared that the fall in silver was only a
momentary accident in a weak market, and not
the permanent effect of lasting causes; that
exports from the silver-using countries would
be stimulated, and imports reduced ; that the
surplus silver would in this way be absorbed,
and even that the old ratio between silver and
gold might be restored, or, at any rate, that
a new and stable ratio between gold and silver
would be established. In forming this judg-

Anticipation s
of the English
econ o m i s t s
regarding the
effects of the
fall in the re-
lative value of
silver.

ment, the nature of the connection hitherto
maintained between gold and silver by the
bimetallic system of France appears to have
been overlooked, and the forecast could only be
justified on the assumption that it was silver
that had fallen in value, and not gold that had
risen. If gold had risen in value owing to
insufficiency of supply compared with the work
which it had to do, the gold prices of commodities would fall in the gold-using countries in
the same proportion in which silver had fallen
relatively to gold, and there would be no stimulus to exports from the silver-using countries, nor check on imports.

So long, however, as gold prices remained
the same, the fall in the relative value of silver
would, no doubt, tend to stimulate exports from
the silver-using countries ; and the stimulus
would continue to have effect until prices in the
silver-using countries had risen by the same
proportion in which the value of silver had
fallen. The fall in silver would also tend to
check imports of merchandise into the silver-
using countries, and would, other things being
equal, tend to increase the import of silver
into those countries.

These antici-
pations not
justified by
the results.
Whether the anticipations that the old ratio
between gold and silver might be restored were
in themselves reasonable or not, they certainly
have not been justified by the result, and we
seem to be as far from the establishment of a
stable ratio between gold and silver as we were
ten years ago. Moreover, an examination of the
economic position of India at the time when
the fall in silver began to occur, and of the
facts of subsequent years, will show that influences were at work which counteracted the
action of the causes with which the English

economists dealt from a purely *à priori* stand-point, and on what appears to me to have been an inadequate appreciation of the facts.

Before considering what the actual facts have been since the fixed ratio between silver and gold was destroyed, it will be convenient to consider what, in accordance with the bime-tallic theory, they might have been expected to be.

What might have been expected according to the bimetallic theory.

If the bimetallic system had not been aban-doned, gold and silver would have continued to divide between them the duty of money in such manner as to preserve the ratio of value at 1 to 15½.

The bimetallic system was, however, aban-doned ; gold was called on to do more work and silver less work.

As compared with the state of affairs under the previously existing bimetallic system, every limitation to the extent to which silver dis-charged the duties of money was necessarily attended by an exactly equal extension of the duties which gold was called on to perform ; for instance, as Germany demonetised and sold the silver of her currency, she was forced to replace it by gold.

Every contraction of the extent to which silver performs the duty of money neces-sarily accom-panied by an exactly equal extension of the duty per-formed by gold.

Besides this permanent alteration in the re-lative extent to which gold and silver discharged the duties of money, there would, in the first instance, be a certain amount of demonetised silver thrown on the market, which would lower the price of silver, and stimulate exports from the silver-using countries until the surplus me-tal had been absorbed by those countries.

Special stimu-lus to exports from silver countries.

When this special supply had been absorbed, the special stimulus to exports would cease, and silver would exchange for gold at rates which would vary from time to time, according to the state of the market, but, on the whole, at rates lower than the old legal ratio.

Illustration of the effects of changing the material of the currency.

As an illustration of this portion of the question, let us assume that there are two nations subject to the conditions assumed to exist in Chapter IV. A population of 1,000,000 has a currency composed of 10,000,000 coins of A metal, and another population of equal numbers has a currency composed of 100,000,000 coins of B metal. The ratio of exchange is 1 to 10.

Let us suppose that $\frac{1}{10}$th of the people using the B metal decide to abandon its use and to substitute A metal. In order to do so, they will find it necessary to export to the nation using the A metal a sufficient quantity of commodities to induce it to part with the required amount of A coins, and their next step will be to replace this wealth as far as possible by purchasing from the persons who continue to use the B metal as many commodities as can be obtained in exchange for the demonetised B metal. When the necessary exchanges have been completed, there will be a population of 1,100,000 using A metal and having a currency of $9\frac{1}{11}$ coins per head, and a population of 900,000 using B metal and having $111\frac{1}{9}$ coins per head. Exports of commodities to the nation which originally used metal A will have been specially stimulated in the process to the amount of the value of 1,000,000 of A coins. Property of this value will have been gained by that nation at the expense of the nation which formerly used the B metal, and the price it has paid for this gain is a lowering of prices in the proportion of 10 to $9\frac{1}{11}$ while the corresponding gain of the persons still using the B metal has been a raising of prices in the proportion of 100 to $111\frac{1}{9}$.

The new ratio of exchange between the two metals which will ultimately be established will be as $9\frac{11}{11}$ to $111\frac{1}{5}$, or as 1 to $12\frac{2}{9}$ instead of as 1 to 10.

It is obvious, then, that the result of alter- ing the proportion of the duty of money dis- charged by gold and silver is— Summary of the results of changing the material of the currency.

(1) A transfer of wealth from one nation to another, this being that temporary stimu- lus to exports of which we have heard so much.

(2) The permanent raising of prices in the country which has lost the wealth.

(3) The permanent lowering of prices in the country which gained the wealth.

(4) A permanent alteration of the rate of exchange between the two countries.

The problem with which we have to deal is not, however, so simple as the hypothetical case above stated, because the nations that were formerly bimetallic did not, when they stopped the free coinage of silver, demonetise and sell their silver coin, and because the United States of America, though possessing a gold standard, have continued, under a special law, to absorb a large amount of silver every year. The special stimulus to exports from the silver countries has been limited to the effect pro- duced by the demonetised silver of Germany, but there is still a stimulus of moderate amount the intensity of which depends upon the re- duced demand for silver in Europe, *plus* the increased production and *minus* the relief given by the Bland Bill. The present case complicat- ed by special considerations.

Briefly, then, the effects which might have been anticipated, in accordance with the bime- tallic theory, were a tendency in gold prices to fall and in silver prices to rise—a stimulus of no great amount to exports from silver countries which would last while Germany was selling her silver, and a snbsequent slight but long-continued stimulus due to the larger supplies of, and reduced demand for, silver.   There never was the least likelihood that the old ratio of 1 to $15\frac{1}{2}$ would be restored unless as the result of legislation, and a stable ratio could not be attained in the future unless by international agreement.   It will also be evident that the future must be darkened and the course of commerce disturbed by the large supplies of silver valued above its market price held by countries that had formerly been bimetallic, and by the essentially provisional nature of the arrangements made by the Bland Bills.

CHAPTER XX.

It has frequently been assumed, in dealing with the question of the effects of the demonetisation of silver in Europe, that the East, and especially India, possesses an unlimited and unaccountable power of absorbing silver. So long as the Indian Mints are the only ones that are open for the coinage of silver, all supplies of that metal that are not wanted for other purposes will, of course, be brought to them to be coined, but it seems to me that there has been much misconception regarding the power of India and the East to absorb silver without the exchange value of silver relatively to gold being greatly reduced, and it is desirable to examine this aspect of the question before proceeding further.

For facility of reference, I give here the figures of the imports into and exports from India, and also the net imports of gold and silver since 1835-36. I have also added the amounts paid in India every year since 1854-55 by the Indian Government in discharge of bills drawn in London :—

[*Millions of Rupees.*]

Official year.	MERCHANDISE.		NET IMPORTS.		
	Imports.	Exports.	Silver.	Gold.	Amount of bills paid in India.
1835–36 ...	48	111	16	3	
1836–37 ...	55	132	13	4	
1837–38 ...	50	112	20	4	
1838–39 ...	52	118	26	3	
1839–40 ...	58	109	17	2	
1840–41 ...	84	135	14	1	
1841–42 ...	78	138	13	2	
1842–43 ...	76	136	30	2	
1843–44 ...	88	173	37	4	
1844–45 ...	108	166	20	7	
1845–46 ...	91	170	9	5	
1846–47 ...	89	154	14	8	
1847–48 ...	86	133	−5	10	
1848–49 ...	83	161	3	13	
1849–50 ...	103	173	13	11	
1850–51 ...	116	182	21	12	
1851–52 ...	122	199	29	13	
1852–53 ...	101	205	46	12	
1853–54 ...	111	193	23	11	
1854–55 ...	127	189	0	7	36
1855–56 ...	139	230	82	25	18
1856–57 ...	142	253	111	21	29
1857–58 ...	153	275	122	28	13
1858–59 ...	217	299	77	44	0
1859–60 ...	243	280	111	43	0
1860–61 ...	235	330	53	42	0
1861–62 ...	223	363	91	52	8
1862–63 ...	226	479	126	68	59
1863–64 ...	271	656	128	89	94
1864–65 ...	282	680	101	98	72
1865–66 ...	296	655	187	57	64
1866–67 (11 months)	290	419	70	38	59
1867–68 ...	357	509	56	46	38
1868–69 ...	360	531	86	52	46
1869–70 ...	329	525	73	56	59
1870–71 ...	345	553	9	23	97
1871–72 ...	321	632	65	36	100
1872–73 ...	319	553	7	25	151
1873–74 ...	338	550	25	14	143
1874–75 ...	362	564	46	19	120
1875–76 ...	389	581	16	15	145
1876–77 ...	374	610	72	2	125
1877–78 ...	415	652	147	5	103
1878–79 ...	378	609	40	−9	175
1879–80 ...	412	672	79	18	180
1880–81 ...	531	746	39	37	182
1881–82 ...	491	820	54	48	221
1882–83 ...	521	835	75	49	184
1883–84 ...	553	881	64	55	229
1884–85 ...	557	832	72	47	160

Silver is not produced to any appreciable extent in India, and consequently that metal must be largely imported to meet ordinary wear and tear of stock, and to provide for the very considerable additions which are made to the population every year.

Ordinary requirements of India as regards silver.

Considering the vast population of India, and the immense stock of silver which she holds, it is probable that in the present day not less than 30 millions of rupees in silver are required yearly to maintain prices at the same level. Large as this sum may appear, it only amounts to about one rupee yearly per 10 persons of the total population supplied with silver by the Indian imports of that metal.

The imports of silver into India from 1835-36 to 1854-55 were very moderate, only 18 millions of rupees yearly, and certainly not more than enough to keep up the currency, provide for increase of population, and meet wear and tear of silver not in circulation.

Moderate imports of silver from 1835-36 to 1854-55 to 1865-66.

From 1855-56 to 1865-66 India imported a very large amount of silver; but imports during this period were mainly due to borrowing to meet expenditure on account of the Mutiny, to the large payments in England by Guaranteed Companies for expenditure in India, and to the special increase in the value of exports due to the demand for cotton in consequence of the American War.

Large imports of silver from 1855-56.

The following table shows in periods of years the net imports of silver since 1855-56, the amount of such imports which was covered by borrowing in one form or another, and the average yearly import in each period, exclusive of borrowing :—

Imports of silver largely due to borrowing.

[*Millions of Rupees.*]

	Net imports of silver.	Amount borrowed in all forms.	Difference.	Average yearly import, exclusive of borrowing.
1855–56 to 1865–66 ...	1,189	690	499	45
1866–67 to 1869-70 ...	285	272	13	–3
1870–71 to 1875–76 ...	168	90	78	13
1876-77 to 1878–79 ...	259	92	167	56
1879–80 to 1884–85 ...	382	65	317	53
Total ...	2,283	1,209	1,074	36

Under the head "Amount borrowed in all
forms" I have shown all borrowing in London
by which the amount of bills drawn on India
was proportionately reduced; all payments in
London by Companies for capital expenditure
in India ; and all silver debt of the Government
of India, payment of interest on which was
transferred from India to London, and which
was presumably borrowed from Europe.

If the sums shown under the two former
heads had not been received, the drawings on
India would have been increased by an equivalent amount, and the exports of silver to
India would, *pro tanto*, have been reduced.

Of the silver debt of India, 206 millions
were transferred to the London register for
payment of interest between 1855-56 to 1884-85.
I have assumed that the latter figure is the
amount of the silver debt incurred during this
period which was borrowed from Europe—an
assumption which is probably under the mark.

It will be seen that from 1855-56 to 1865-66
India imported annually 108 millions of rupees ;
but that if we deduct the imports due to borrowing, India imported only 45 millions of

rupees annually during this period, notwithstanding the special impulse given to imports of silver by the American War.

From 1866-67 to 1875-76 India imported very little silver indeed, except what she borrowed.

From 1876-77 to 1884-85 India has imported a considerable quantity of silver apart from the imports due to borrowing.

The conclusion to be drawn from these figures is that from 1855-56 to 1865-66 India imported silver largely owing to borrowing and from special causes; that in 1866-67 her supply of silver had in this way been raised above what may be called equilibrium; that consequently from 1866-67 to 1875-76 she would have imported very little silver but for further borrowing; that the borrowing from 1866-67 to 1875-76 served to maintain the Indian currency above equilibrium; and that India might have been expected for some time after 1875-76 to import very little silver, unless under the influence of borrowing or other special causes.

The total amount of silver imported into India from 1855-56 to 1884-85 and *paid for* comes to 36 millions of rupees yearly—an amount not greatly in excess of what India requires to keep prices at the same level; and a large portion of this amount was paid for by the great increase in the value of exports during the American War.

Apart from borrowing, the imports of silver have been moderate.

But although India has, apart from borrowing, only imported 36 millions of rupees yearly since 1855-56, I do not assert that she would only have imported this amount if there had been no borrowing. The wants of India in the matter of silver have been largely supplied by borrowing since 1855-56; and if they had not been so supplied, she would probably have imported more than 36 millions of rupees yearly, paying for the excess either by increasing her exports, or reducing her imports, of merchandise.

The figures which I have given, however, entirely dispose of the assertions so frequently made, that India is a country which from some inexplicable cause has absorbed, and will continue indefinitely to absorb, any quantity of silver without economic disturbance.

Improbability of very large imports of silver in future unless under the stimulus of special causes.

India requires, and under all ordinary circumstances would import, 30 millions of rupees yearly, and may possibly take double that amount; but beyond this figure there is little likelihood that she will go, unless there should be large borrowing on the part of Government, or unless some abnormal cause should come into play, such as that which led to the unprecedented increase in the value of cotton exported from India during the American War. No doubt cheaper freight to Europe stimulates exports, and the extension of irrigation and construction of railways enable more produce to be brought to the ports for export; but there is a limit to the surplus produce which India can spare, and the payment of interest on money already borrowed, as well as the general increase of the home charges of the Government of India, swell the drawings of the Secretary of State, and tend to reduce the imports of silver. Moreover, the supply of silver has been forced and maintained above equilibrium in the past by borrowing; and if the stimulus of special causes were removed, India would probably prefer to take merchandise rather than silver.

It seems, therefore, to be in the highest degree improbable that, apart from borrowing and other special causes, such as a further heavy fall in exchange, India is at all likely to take more than 60 millions of rupees yearly in future.

CHAPTER XXI.

The stimulus to exports and check on imports would necessarily be attended with a rise in the silver prices of both exports and imports.

THOSE who held that the fall in the relative value of silver would stimulate exports from the silver-using countries, and check imports into them, based their argument on the assumption that, owing to the fall in the relative value of silver, the gold countries could afford to give more silver for commodities imported from the silver countries, and that the silver countries would be forced to give more silver for the articles produced in the gold countries, or, in other words, that the prices, measured in silver, of both exports and imports would rise.

The contention was perfectly sound on the assumption that it was silver that had fallen and not gold that had risen, and that gold prices would remain the same as before in the gold-using countries.

According to this theory, the increase in exports and decrease in imports of merchandise, and the correspondingly large imports of silver, would continue until prices had risen in the silver countries proportionately to the fall of silver as compared with gold. When equilibrium was restored in this way, the special impulse to exports and the special check on imports would cease, and exchange between the gold and silver countries would take place according to the ordinary laws.

Let us consider whether these anticipations have been justified by the facts.

If events had followed the course anticipated, we should find in the first instance an increase in the prices of exports, which would be permanently maintained, and would lead for a time to a large increase in the quantities exported. In connection with this matter, I would call attention to Appendix A, which shows the prices of the principal articles of export at Calcutta since 1873. It shows very little rise in any year since 1873, and a large decrease in 1885. From this table I have prepared with some difficulty the following table of index numbers for 13 of the principal articles :—

Prices in silver of Indian exports have not risen.

1873	...	...	...	1600
1874	...	...	...	1729
1875	...	...	...	1491
1876	...	...	...	1519
1877	...	...	...	1634
1878	...	...	...	1645
1879	...	...	...	1652
1880	...	...	...	1765
1881	...	...	...	1584
1882	...	...	...	1530
1883	...	...	...	1453
1884	...	...	...	1607
1885	...	...	...	1364

The numbers show a good deal of fluctuation, but on the whole the course is steadily downwards; the high index numbers in certain years being due to famine rates for rice in Calcutta and excessive fluctuations in the prices of one or two articles of no great importance.

A further indication of the course of prices may be obtained by observing the relation between the recorded values and quantities, according to the Customs returns, of articles exported from India.

Indication of prices afforded by recorded values and quantities of imports and exports.

The table of export prices on p. 100 has
been obtained by comparing the recorded
values and quantities of articles exported.

These figures show no general increase in
the prices of exports.

It is clear then that the anticipation of a
stimulus to exports attended by a permanent
rise in price has not been fulfilled.

Prices in sil-
ver of imports
into India have
not risen. I need not deal specially with imports into
India.   If the reader will turn to page 78,
he will see that for 1873 Mr. Giffen's *datum* for
export prices of English, commodities (65·8) required to be increased by 19·93, raising it to
85·73, and that for 1883 it required to be reduced by 5·95, bringing it down to 59·85 ; so
that there was a fall between 1873 and 1883
in the gold prices of English exports from
85·73 to 59·85, or of rather more than 30 per
cent.   But 1873 was a year of remarkable inflation of price.   If we compare 1875 with
1883, we find a fall from 74·47 to 59·85, or
more than 19 per cent.   Between 1875 and
1883, therefore, the gold prices of exports from
England (and consequently of imports into
India) fell by an amount almost exactly equivalent to the total fall in the value of silver as
compared with gold.   Since 1883 the prices of
English exports have fallen still further, and
we arrive at the remarkable fact that, apart
from the temporary inflation of 1873, the gold
prices of English exports, and therefore of
Indian imports, have fallen more than silver
has fallen in relation to gold ; that the silver
prices of Indian imports are now lower, and
not higher ; and that the check on imports
into India, which was expected to be caused
by the rise in silver prices of imports, has had
no existence in reality.

The same conclusion follows from an examination of the prices of the chief articles of import as determined from the values and quantities of imports recorded in the Customs returns.

The table on p. 101 shows clearly that there has been no such rise in the silver price of imports as we should have expected if silver had fallen in value in relation to commodities.

PRICES OF EXPORTS.

		Average of 5 years ending 1873-74.	1874-75.	1875-76.	1876-77.	1877-78.	1878-79.	1879-80.	1880-81.	1881-82.	1882-83.	1883-84.	1884-85.
		Rs.	Rs.	Rs.	Rs.	Rs.	Rs.	Rs.	Rs.	Rs.	Rs.	Rs.	Rs.
Rice	.. per cwt.	2·7	2·8	2·6	2·9	3·8	4·3	3·8	3·4	2·9	2·7	3·1	3·3
Wheat	.. "	4·2	4·6	3·6	3·5	4·5	4·9	5·1	4·4	4·3	4·3	4·2	4·0
Tea	.. 10 lbs.	8·6	9·2	8·9	9·4	9·1	9·1	8·0	8·6	7·4	6·4	6·8	6·3
Cotton	.. cwt.	33·2	27·2	26·5	25·8	26·4	26·7	28·2	29·1	26·5	26·0	24·1	26·2
Raw hides..	.. "	..	..	31·4	31·2	28·7	26·0	27·8	31·5	32·0	32·3	34·0	34·4
Raw jute ..	.. "	6·2	5·9	5·4	5·8	6·5	6·3	6·5	6·8	6·7	5·6	6·5	5·6
Linseed ..	.. "	5·0	5·0	5·3	5·4	5·9	6·2	6·5	6·2	5·8	5·2	5·4	5·6
Rape ..	.. "	4·5	4·5	4·8	5·5	6·0	6·3	6·2	5·4	5·3	5·6	6·2	5·9
Til ..	.. "	6·0	6·0	5·6	6·6	7·3	7·7	7·2	6·9	6·3	6·3	6·9	7·3
Wool ..	.. 100 lbs.	38·7	45·1	46·0	44·8	40·9	39·8	41·5	44·8	37·7	36·7	37·7	37·7
Cotton twist and yarn	.. "	52·8	52·4	42·9	46·3	43·7	41·6	42·9	47·7	44·5	40·0	38·6	37·0
Cotton piece-goods, grey	.. 100 yds.	..	..	15·7	15·5	14·1	13·2	12·5	12·7	12·2	11·3	11·2	10·9

PRICES OF IMPORTS.

		Average of 5 years during 1873-74.	1874-75.	1875-76.	1876-77.	1877-78.	1878-79.	1879-80.	1880-81.	1881-82.	1882-83.	1883-84.	1884-65.
		Rs.	Rs.	Rs.	Rs.	Rs.	Rs.	Rs.	Rs.	Rs.	Rs.	Rs.	Rs.
Coal ...	per ton.	16·4	18·9	17·2	17·8	16·7	18·6	19·2	17·8	15·9	15·7	16·2	16·9
Cotton twist and yarn	100 lbs.	84·5	85·1	87·6	82·2	78·8	83·9	82·7	80·6	79·6	75·3	76·4	75·0
Piece-goods, grey ...	100 yds.	12·7	13·1	12·4	12·0	11·7	11·2	11·4	11·6	11·8	11·7	11·1	10·8
Piece-goods, coloured ...	„	15·7	16·2	18·3	17·8	16·3	16·1	15·8	16·2	15·6	15·6	15·5	15·0
Unwrought copper ...	cwt.	42·9	40·7	52·1	54·2	47·9	44·3	42·5	42·7	42·5	42·0	42·1	37·3
Wrought iron, bar ...	„	...	...	7·1	6·3	5·3	5·7	5·4	5·2	5·3	5·5	5·3	4·9
Unwrought tin ...	„	44·9	45·0	40·7	49·0	45·7	43·4	48·2	57·3	62·9	64·8	60·3	54·0
Betel nuts ...	100 lbs.	...	...	6·5	8·0	7·9	9·8	9·0	8·3	8·1	9·1	11·2	10·9
Pepper ...	„	...	...	20·9	20·7	18·8	17·0	17·7	19·1	21·3	23·9	28·2	32·9
Sugar, refined ...	cwt.	12·6	13·0	14·6	15·7	16·8	16·1	16·4	16·4	16·1	16·2	15·7	13·3
Umbrellas ...	Set of 10	7·6	7·5	8·0	7·6	7·7	7·4	7·2	7·4	7·1	6·9	7·1	7·4
Raw silk ...	lb.	3·7	3·5	2·8	3·1	3·2	3·1	3·4	4·2	4·3	4·5	4·4	4·1
Silk piece-goods ...	100 yds.	109·3	100·0	87·3	110·8	100·2	111·9	102·5	101·1	108·0	104·5	108·1	109·6

CHAPTER XXII.

THE prices with which we have dealt in the preceding chapter have been prices at the coast. It will not be uninteresting to consider, so far as the means at our disposal permit, what has been the course of prices in the interior of the country. The case of imports need not be specially considered. Imports are cheaper at the coast than they formerly were ; and as the cost of carriage into the interior of the country has been growing less year by year, we may feel sure that imports are cheaper in the in_terior than they have been at any former period.

The general question of the rise or fall of prices in the interior of India is one of much difficulty. Prices vary so much from time to time, and from place to place, in a country so vast, and which has long suffered from defective means of communication and defective rainfall inducing local famine, that, unless there had been a marked fall or rise, it would be hopeless to attempt to discover the working of a general law among so many discordant elements.

The course of the prices of exports at the coast would not justify the opinion that there has been any considerable rise of prices in the interior of India, though doubtless the improvement in means of communication, and especially the construction of railways, would tend to raise the average of prices by raising prices in

those tracts in which they had hitherto been
kept at a low figure by the impossibility of finding a market for surplus produce. The question of the rise or fall in prices of the principal
articles of food has recently been investigated
by Mr. J. E. O'Conor of the Financial Department of the Government of India, and the
following figures at which he has arrived after
careful inquiry possess a special interest at the
present time. I have thought it sufficient to
give the prices for five of the principal food-
grains, the course of prices of other food-grains
being the same.

Seers per one rupee. *

Wheat.	North-Western Provinces and Oudh. 11 districts	Punjab. 6 districts.	Central Provinces. 3 districts.	Hyderabad Territory. 3 districts	Bombay. 8 districts.
Average of 1861-67 (7 years) ...	21·17	21·99	27·3	12·45	11·95
Average of 1868-74 (7 years) ...	17·57	17·29	23·52	12·41	12·33
Average of 1875-81 (7 years) ...	18·65	18·19	24·81	13·14	11·71
Average of 1882-84 (3 years) ...	18·82	22·22	23·34	17·61	14·31

Seers per one rupee.

Rice.	Bengal. 14 districts	Madras. 7 districts.	Central Provinces. 3 districts.	Burma. 7 districts
Average of 1861-67 (7 years)	22·41	12·25	21·1	17·09
„ 1868-74 („)	21·41	14·93	19·07	18·35
„ 1875-81 („)	18·71	12·35	19·96	15·07
„ 1882-84 (3 years)	19·92	15·61	21·88	15·22

* Prices are here shown according to the Indian system. The
English reader should recollect that the larger the quantity of grain
that can be purchased for a rupee, the lower is the price of that grain.
A seer is 2½ lbs.

Seers per rupee:

*Jowar.**	Bombay.	Central Provinces.	Punjab.	North-western Provinces.	Madras.
	9 districts.	2 districts.	2 districts.	11 districts	5 districts.
Average of 1861-67 (7 years) ...	17·37	22·36	28·54	25·18	20·03
Average of 1868-74 (7 years) ...	18·86	21·74	23·01	21·57	26·15
Average of 1875-81 (7 years) ...	17·33	24·98	23·68	24·92	19·9
Average of 1882-84 (3 years) ...	20 21	27·99	33·46	27·92	29·8

Seers per rupee.

Barley.	Oudh.	North-West Provinces.	Punjab.
	3 districts.	8 districts.	6 districts.
Average of 1861-67 (7 years) ...	31·36	29·43	38·08
„ 1868-74 („) ..	23·53	25·18	27·36
„ 1875-81 („) ...	27·78	26·46	27·36
„ 1882-84 (3 years) ...	28·45	27·19	35·24

Seers per rupee.

*Bajra.**	Bombay.	Madras.	North-West Provinces and Oudh.	Punjab.
	9 districts.	5 districts.	11 districts	6 districts.
Average of 1861-67 (7 years)	15·57	20·85	23·22	25·98
„ 1868-74 („)	17·32	25·19	19·39	20 53
„ 1875-81 („)	16·	20·45	22·01	21·16
„ 1882-84 (3 years)	18·39	29 95	24·9	27·78

Mr. O'Conor's figures show very clearly that
there has been no general rise of the price of

---

* A species of millet.

food-grains in India. The harvests of 1882-83-84 have been better than the average, and the cheapening of grain from this cause has more than counteracted the effects of the opening up of districts which formerly could not send their surplus produce to the coast for export.

I have also examined tables showing for several provinces the cost of work done in successive years by the Irrigation Department. The Irrigation Department was chosen, because its work is generally carried on at a distance from the great centres of population, and its rates are not affected by so many special disturbing causes as in the case of other branches of the Indian Public Works Department. I found the general course of prices to be the same in all provinces, and it is unnecessary, therefore, to print the tables for more than one province—the Punjab.

Prices and wages in the Irrigation Branch of the Public Works Department.

The figures given on p. 109 are the average rates for the province ; and as work is not being carried on every year in the same places, the average does not, in all cases, fairly represent the whole province ; but the figures show very fairly what the general course of wages has been, and they are conclusive as regards a large and steady rise in the wages of skilled labour, such as that of masons, bricklayers, carpenters, and blacksmiths—a result which might have been anticipated from the construction of railways, canals, and other great public works.

Wages of skilled labour have largely risen.

On the other hand, the rates for earthwork show that, away from the great centres of trade and industry, there has been no very marked improvement in the wages of unskilled labour —a result probably due, in some degree, to in-

Wages of unskilled labour have not risen in the same proportion.

crease of population in a country remarkably deficient in manufacturing industry.

As a further test in dealing with the question of a rise in wages, I have obtained statements showing, since 1855, the rates of pay of postmen and runners employed by the Post Office, which are given in Appendix B.

Wages of postmen have largely risen. The rates of pay of postmen have, it will be seen, increased very largely ; but this increase is chiefly due to a change in the nature of their work, which has become of a more responsible nature, and requires greater intelligence for its performance.

In 1855 the postmen were only required to deliver letters, and many of them could not read even the vernacular language. They now pay money orders, and those drawing the higher rates of pay are expected to be able to read English as well as the vernacular language.

The statement of the pay given to postmen in successive years affords, however, a good illustration of the manner in which a demand for a higher kind of labour is gradually growing up in India as its organisation becomes more complex.

Moderate increase in wages of postal runners. The statement showing the pay of postal runners is of special value. The runners are the men who carry the mail from stage to stage where no other means of conveyance is available. Their pay represents the wages of the lowest class of unskilled labour, and the rates given are the lowest market rates for which their services could be obtained. The average rates of pay in different years have been as follow :—

Monthly wages.

Rs.

1855	·	·	·	·	·	4·05
1860	·	·	·	·	·	4·56
1865	·	·	·	·	·	4·95
1870	·	·	·	·	·	5·20
1875	·	·	·	·	·	5 14
1880	·	·	·	·	·	5 24
1885	·	·	·	·	·	5·35

These figures show conclusively that the market rates for unskilled labour away from the great centres have not increased in any considerable degree since 1870. It will be observed that the figures of the Postal Department fully corroborate those of the Public Works Department, so far as they go; there is an increased demand for, and higher wages are given to, skilled and intelligent workmen; but there has not been the same improvement in the position of ordinary labourers, taking them as a class and not confining our attention to the great cities, where the wages of unskilled labour have certainly increased in a material degree.

We thus see that the prices of exports at the coast have not increased, that the prices of food-grains in the interior are not higher than they were, though this may be in some measure due to the good harvests of recent years, and that, away from the great centres, the wages of unskilled labour have risen very little. On the other hand, there has been a large rise in the wages of skilled labour; the number of skilled labourers is, unfortunately, inconsiderable as compared with the number of unskilled labourers, and on the whole the rise in wages has been very moderate.

Summary.

The final conclusion can only be that the fall in the value of silver as compared with gold

has, up to the present date, not had any considerable effect in raising prices or wages in India ;
though there can be no doubt as to its influence
in preventing a fall.

THE PANJAB.

Cost.	1862.	1863.	1864.	1865.	1866.	1867.	1868.	1869.	1870.	1871.	1872.
	Ans.	Ans.	Ans.	Ans.	Ans.	Ans.	Ans.	Ans.	Ans.	Ans.	Ans.
Earthwork per 1,000 cubic feet ...	42	32	33	41	40	48	56	42	50	53	40
Masonry per 100 cubic feet ...	236	230	259	287	232	316	296	259	299	298	322
Woodwork per cubic foot ...	24	22	24	24	32	40	44	25	41	...	20
Country ironwork per maund ...	176	176	208	253	276	288	308	304	312	293	349
Bricks per 1,000 ...	124	112	160	120	120	160	160	184	192	192	176
Lime per 100 cubic feet ...	237	289	245	377	336	360	264	240	288	277	362

THE PANJAB (continued.)

Cost.	1873.	1874.	1875.	1876.	1877.	1878.	1879.	1880.	1881.	1882.	1883.	1884.
	Ans.	Ans.	Ans.	Ans.	Ans.	Ans.	Ans.	Ans.	Ans.	Ans.	Ans.	Ans.
Earthwork per 1,000 cubic feet ...	41	48	37	32	40	51	54	54	58	49	52	39
Masonry per 100 cubic feet ...	278	322	320	330	312	348	320	343	344	376	343	323
Woodwork per cubic foot ...	...	41	35	...	58	45	34	36	36	39	24	23
Country ironwork per maund ...	272	305	264	260	993	210	296	320	334	292	277	280
Bricks per 1,000 ...	204	192	192	192	192	192	132	160	160	160	160	168
Lime per 100 cubic feet ...	344	384	400	400	400	372	305	391	348	352	352	360

CHAPTER XXIII.

IT has been shown in Chapter **XXII** that there has not, to say the least, been any rise in the silver prices of exports from India, nor in the silver prices of imports into India.

There has not, therefore, been any special stimulus to exports or check on imports due to a rise in silver prices. Silver prices of exports at the coast have remained nearly the same, with however a tendency to fall in very recent years.

The change which has actually taken place has been a fall in gold prices, both of exports and imports.

We will now proceed to consider what the actual course of the import and export trade of India has been since the fall in the rate of exchange ; and to do so with advantage it will be necessary to consider the course of trade for some years previous to the date on which this fall began to declare itself.

The figures of the import and export trade have been already given at page 90, and need not be repeated.

General course of Indian foreign trade. Examining these figures, we find that from 1855-56 to 1861-62 there was a large, and, on the whole, steady growth of exports.

During the same period imports also increased, mainly owing to increased imports of cotton goods from England.

The American War gave an enormous stimulus to the Indian cotton trade from 1862-63 to 1865-66, and prices rose so high that the value of the raw cotton exported in 1864-65 was nearly seven times the value of the cotton exports of 1859-60, although the quantity was increased by little more than 50 per cent.

Increase in value of exports of cotton owing to American War.

During the same period the imports of merchandise showed a steady and considerable increase, but the increase did not at all approach the value of the increase in exports. During the four years 1862-63 to 1865-66 India imported no less than 542 million rupees in silver and 312 million rupees worth of gold, while only taking merchandise in excess of the figure of the years immediately preceding to the amount of 157 million rupees in the four years. Moreover, nearly one-half of the increase in the value of merchandise imported was due to the higher price which India had to pay for manufactured cotton goods, of which the quantity imported actually fell off.

Payments for cotton exported largely taken in gold and silver.

The result is perhaps not other than might have been expected, seeing that a sudden influx of wealth among the Indian peasantry could hardly lead at once to a greatly increased demand for foreign luxuries of which they had little or no knowledge. Gold and silver appeal to all men's feelings, and in gold and silver the Indian people preferred to receive the value of their cotton.

From 1866-67 to 1874-75 there was a steady, but not very great, growth of the export trade. The quantity of raw cotton exported every

Moderate increase of exports from 1866-67 to 1874-75.

year from 1866-67 to 1874-75 remained nearly
constant, but its value declined largely. On
the other hand, both the value and quantity
of the indigo, rice, jute, seeds, and tea trade
increased steadily. The famine of 1874 affected both the rice and indigo trades very in-
juriously, and the total exports of the year
would have been low but for a large export of
cotton.

No increase of imports of merchandise during this time.   The total value of the exports of 1874-75
exceeded that of 1867-68 by only 55 millions
of rupees, and as the Secretary of State had
been increasing his drawings, there could not
be any considerable increase in imports of
merchandise. In fact, the value of the imports of merchandise in 1874-75 only exceeded that of 1867-68 by 5 millions of rupees,
while the imports of silver fell off by 10 millions of rupees.

Moderate in-crease of ex-ports from 1874-75 to 1878-79.   From 1874-75 to 1878-79 there was no very
great increase of exports, the figures for these
years being 564, 581, 610, 652 and 609 millions of rupees. During this period the imports
of merchandise were almost stationary, but the
imports of silver were very large in the years
1876-77 and 1877-78, and the imports of gold
were trifling during the whole period. We
see, then, that from 1874-75 to 1878-79 there
was no remarkable stimulus of exports, and
consequently there could be no large increase
of total imports, including silver and gold.
These years were affected by the great Madras
famine, and the combined effect of the famine
and the rise in the price of gold was largely to
reduce the imports of gold.

Large increase of exports after 1878-79.   After 1878-79 there was a large increase in
the export trade, and the exports of 1884-85
exceeded those of 1874-75 by 268 millions of

rupees. The following tables show the quantities and values of the articles to which this great increase is due. I have included cotton in the table on page 114, for, though its value in 1884-85 is less than in 1874-75, it is very much greater than it was in 1878-79.

When the exports began to increase after 1878-79, the imports of all kinds also increased, for although the Secretary of State largely increased his drawings, the increase was far less than the increase in exports.

Large increase of imports of merchandise after 1878-79.

The imports of 1884-85 exceeded those of 1874-75 by 195 millions of rupees.

The tables on page 115 show the quantities and value of the chief articles of which the import has largely increased.

QUANTITIES.

		Average of 5 years ending 1873-74	1874-75.	1875-76.	1876-77.	1877-78.	1878-79.	1879-80.	1880-81.	1881-82.	1882-33.	1883-84.	1884-85.
Raw cotton	cwt.	5,250,475	5,600,086	5,010,785	4,557,914	3,560,568	2,966,569	3,948,476	4,541,548	5,629,544	6,171,066	5,987,278	5,669,713
Cotton twist	lb.	2,461,774	3,615,945	7,021,170	8,766,249	16,534,728	22,087,156	26,704,713	27,527,186	31,533,733	46,240,953	61,221,002	66,855,602
Cotton piece-goods	yds.	59,837,728	68,981,199	66,084,708	71,585,356	73,476,531	81,062,102	81,251,197	88,510,099	96,126,924	111,741,751	129,955,190	109,936,577
Indigo	cwt.	109,505	81,466	110,392	100,384	120,605	105,051	100,935	116,870	159,369	141,041	168,590	154,629
Rice	,,	17,168,818	16,940,642	20,090,397	19,548,741	18,211,027	20,633,637	21,908,588	26,769,355	28,519,437	31,029,721	26,831,715	21,702,430
Wheat	,,	622,759	1,073,655	2,510,991	5,586,604	6,373,168	1,066,720	2,201,515	7,444,375	19,901,005	14,193,763	21,001,412	15,850,881
Hides and skins	,,			636,715	654,321	905,972	809,329	958,723	812,590	815,490	866,450	916,318	1,010,869
Raw jute	,,	5,291,588	5,493,957	5,206,570	4,533,255	5,450,276	6,021,382	6,680,670	5,809,815	7,510,314	10,348,909	7,017,985	8,368,686
Manufactured jute number of gunny bags		6,127,301	8,010,824	19,263,513	32,859,545	26,400,689	45,354,044	55,906,731	52,386,227	42,072,819	60,737,651	63,645,934	82,779,207
Seeds	cwt.	4,692,207	6,074,756	10,507,404	9,583,170	12,187,619	7,211,790	7,246,182	10,303,776	10,482,512	18,147,989	17,357,884	18,250,931
Sugar	,,	(a) 300,418	559,267	507,403	1,144,191	908,250	368,540	973,242	644,531	988,341	1,428,360	1,777,137	1,251,059
Tea	lbs.	16,057,546	21,392,760	24,561,826	27,925,800	33,656,961	34,800,027	38,404,632	46,918,539	49,255,342	53,233,345	60,473,113	65,147,897

VALUES. *Millions of rupees.*

	Average of 5 years ending 1873-74.	1874-75.	1875-76.	1876-77.	1877-78.	1878-79.	1879-80.	1880-81.	1881-82.	1882-83.	1883-84.	1884-85.
Raw cotton	174.1	152.6	132.9	117.5	93.9	79.1	111.5	132.4	149.4	160.6	144.0	139.0
Cotton twist	1.4	2.0	3.2	4.3	7.4	9.4	11.6	13.3	14.3	18.7	20.1	25.1
Indigo piece-goods	12.0	14.0	13.4	14.3	14.4	15.2	14.8	10.6	18.0	20.0	22.2	20.0
Indigo	34.1	25.8	28.8	29.0	34.9	29.6	29.5	35.7	45.1	39.1	46.4	40.7
Rice	45.6	46.7	52.4	57.4	68.0	88.2	83.4	69.7	82.5	81.4	83.3	71.3
Wheat	2.7	4.9	9.1	19.8	29.7	5.2	11.2	32.8	86.2	60.9	89.0	63.2
Hides and skins	23.6	26.8	29.4	30.0	37.6	31.0	37.4	37.4	39.5	44.4	46.7	49.4
Raw jute	32.6	32.5	28.1	26.4	35.2	38.0	43.7	39.3	50.3	58.5	45.9	46.6
Manufactured jute (gunny bags)	1.5	4.4	4.6	6.5	7.3	10.4	11.3	10.9	10.8	14.3	12.6	14.1
Seeds	24.9	32.4	54.6	53.2	73.0	46.8	47.8	63.9	60.6	100.9	100.9	107.5
Sugar	3.6	2.3	3.8	10.0	8.5	3.5	2.9	5.1	7.2	9.9	11.3	7.9
Tea	14.1	19.6	21.3	26.2	30.6	31.7	30.7	31.0	36.6	37.4	41.3	41.4
Total	371.3	303.9	382.7	396.5	442.6	389.9	437.5	509.7	601.8	621.9	666.0	622.2

(a) Figures defective, quantity for a value of Rs. 2,650,000 not being available.

Note.—In the case of cotton twist, cotton piece-goods, and hides and skins, the values for five years ending 1873-74 are based on tariff valuations, which were almost always below the real value.

QUANTITIES.

	Average of 5 years ending 1873-74.	1874-75.	1875-76.	1876-77.	1877-78.	1878-79.	1879-80.	1880-81.	1881-82.	1882-83.	1883-84.	1884-85.
Coal .. .. tons.	329,617		403,060	540,332	609,833	479,790	606,700	729,068	648,201	662,347	712,900	757,673
Cotton twist .. lbs.	32,467,731	37,097,200	31,927,340	33,270,208	56,196,661	33,145,651	33,212,952	45,877,379	40,763,209	44,860,883	45,378,516	44,801,397
Cotton piece-goods yds.	976,679,840	1,039,036,365	994,813,758	1,187,032,725	1,359,089,444	1,127,875,550	1,333,797,549	1,774,336,200	1,623,333,976	1,641,674,763	1,722,378,548	1,732,233,839
Manufactured me-tals .. .. cwt.	1,356,309	1,886,826	2,543,615	2,991,321	3,200,767	3,021,436	1,800,004	3,444,491	3,961,775	4,324,640	4,858,410	4,855,700
Oils .. .. gals.			751,440	642,890	2,825,358	4,337,215	6,268,404	10,286,404	10,234,041	21,867,521	14,481,035	27,786,053
Silk piece-goods .. yds.	4,003,113	6,970,667	7,770,283	5,082,405	7,097,739	7,350,804	7,467,814	11,058,163	10,737,731	9,518,119	9,627,673	10,221,778
Sugar .. .. cwt.	470,679	395,715	613,151	258,105	475,105	923,381	652,009	986,321	775,982	672,672	736,900	1,616,874
Woollen piece-goods .. yds.	5,453,257	5,043,281	7,859,961	7,164,904	7,884,787	8,041,570	6,188,621	12,250,488	9,799,843	7,465,948	10,267,963	11,316,862

VALUES. [Millions of rupees.]

	Average of 5 years ending 1873-74.	1874-75.	1875-76.	1876-77.	1877-78.	1878-79.	1879-80.	1880-81.	1881-82.	1882-83.	1883-84.	1884-85.
Coal ..	5·5	9·0	6·8	9·6	10·2	9·0	11·7	13·2	10·3	10·4	11·7	12·9
Cotton twist ..	27·5	31·6	27·9	27·3	28·5	27·8	27·5	37·0	32·2	33·8	34·7	33·6
Cotton piece-goods ..	147·7	169·2	161·8	157·4	169·7	138·1	165·8	224·0	204·3	209·8	211·8	207·1
Machinery ..	5·9	11·9	14·4	9·6	8·7	8·9	6·4	8·1	12·7	13·9	8·4	15·7
Manufactured metals ..	24·1	26·1	33·1	37·2	37·3	38·7	34·4	38·5	35·8	48·3	58·7	49·7
Oils ..	·5	1·1	·7	3·8	3·0	3·7	5·5	5·3	5·6	10·5	6·5	12·3
Silk piece-goods ..	4·4	7·0	6·8	5·6	7·1	8·2	7·7	11·8	11·1	8·9	10·4	11·2
Railway material ..	9·1	7·8	10·8	11·9	17·3	14·9	15·3	27·4	22·4	20·3	28·7	28·3
Sugar ..	6·0	5·2	9·0	4·0	8·0	14·8	10·7	16·1	12·4	10·9	11·5	21·4
Woollen piece-goods ..	5·0	5·0	8·6	7·5	8·0	7·8	8·2	12·6	10·7	8·6	11·1	10·9

Note.—The values for the five years ending 1873-74, as recorded in the trade returns, for cotton twist, cotton piece-goods, metals, oils, and sugar, are based on tariff valuations. Speaking generally, the real values were almost always in excess of the tariff valuations.

E x p o r t s not
specially sti-
m u l a ted by
rise of prices. We now see that when the fall in silver first
occurred there was no remarkable increase in
exports.   After 1878-79 there was a very great
increase in exports, but this increase was not due
to depreciation of silver, because the silver
prices of exports had not risen.   The increase in
exports was due, in fact, to the opening of the
Suez Canal, to the reduced cost of sea carriage,
and to good harvests, coupled with the opening
out of the country by means of railways, which
not merely enabled produce to be conveyed more
cheaply to the coast, but even in some instances
rendered it possible, for the first time, for the
producer to find a market for his surplus produce.   We shall see hereafter that the fall in
the relative value of silver was not without its
influence on this result; but that fall, it cannot
be too strongly repeated, could only have stimulated exports by increasing their price in silver ;
and, as it has not done so, it cannot have been
the chief cause of the increased exports.

The English economists expected that imports into India would be checked by the increase in their silver prices.   There has, in
Imports not
c h e c k ed by
rise in prices. fact, been no such increase in prices, and imports have grown steadily.   The fall in gold
prices has more than counterbalanced the fall in
the relative value of silver, and the people of
India now get their imports more cheaply, even
under a silver standard, than they formerly
did, and the large increase of exports has
enabled them to increase their imports, notwithstanding the heavy amounts drawn by the
Secretary of State every year to meet the
growing home expenditure of the Government
of India.

CHAPTER XXIV.

NO SPECIAL FLOW OF SILVER TO INDIA SINCE 1873.

W ITH a view to examine still further the question of the depreciation of the Indian currency, I have prepared the following table, which shows the proportion in which Indian imports were divided between merchandise, gold, and silver, at different periods :—

No consider-able substitu-tion of im-ports of silver for imports of merchand i s e after the fall in the relative value of silver.

[*Millions of rupees.*]

Periods.		Average yearly imports, including gold and silver.	Percentage merchan-dise.	Percentage silver.	Percentage gold.
1855-56 to 1865-66	...	380	58·0	28·4	13·6
1866-67 to 1872-73	...	423	78·3	12·4	9·3
1873-74 to 1878-79	...	441	85·2	13·1	1·7
1879-80 to 1884-85	...	617	82·8	10·3	6·9

It will be observed that from 1855-56 to 1865-66 the percentage of silver imported by India was very high, while the percentage of gold was also high, and the precentage of merchandise was low. This period includes the years when the value of Indian cotton had risen so largely, and also covers several years in which London drawings on India had practically ceased.

As already explained, the Indian people preferred at this time to take silver and gold rather than merchandise. During the next period, from 1866-73 to 1872-73, the stimulus of high prices for cotton was withdrawn, and total imports increased very slightly. The proportion of merchandise making up the total imports however largely increased, while the percentage of gold fell largely, and the percentage of silver was considerably less than half what it had been.

If we take now the period 1873-74 to 1878-79, we find that the yearly average of imports was only slightly in excess of that of the preceding period. This result might seem at first sight to confirm the opinion of those who held that the fall in silver would discourage imports into India, but examination shows that it does not do so. The contention of the English economists was that the imports of merchandise would be discouraged and the imports of silver stimulated, and not that the aggregate imports of all kinds would be checked. In fact, as imports depend on exports, and as exports would be stimulated, it would necessarily follow that total imports also would be stimulated, the stimulus being, however, confined to the import of silver.

The exports during the period 1873-74 to 1878-79 averaged 594 millions of rupees yearly, as against 532 millions yearly from 1866-67 to 1872-73. The drawings of the Secretary of State, however, were high during the years 1873-74 to 1878-79, and the excess drawings just covered the increase in exports. For this reason there could be no increase in total imports. If the fall in the rate of exchange had any effect on imports, it could only be by reducing the imports of merchandise and gold, and increasing the imports of silver. but we find that India only imported during this period a very slightly larger proportion of silver than before, and that the falling off in the imports of gold was counterbalanced by an increase in the imports of merchandise. It can readily be understood that when gold first rose in price as compared with silver, a people so conservative and ignorant as the inhabitants of India hesitated to purchase it, imagining, no doubt, that the rise was temporary; and doubtless the distress caused by the Madras famine also affected the imports of gold. The falling off in the imports of gold was not, however, made good by an increase in the imports of silver. The percentage of silver imported increased only by ·7, while the percentage of merchandise increased by 6·9.

No special or injurious stimulus to Indian exports in the period 1873-74 to 1878-79 due to the fall in the value of silver relatively to gold.

We therefore see that when silver first fell in value as compared with gold, there was no extraordinary development of exports, and the percentage of total imports taken in the form of silver was almost the same as before. In other words, there is barely a trace of that reduction in imports of merchandise and increase in the imports of silver which the English economists anticipated.

From 1879-80 the value of the average annual exports rose to 798 millions. A portion of the increase met the increased drawings of the Secretary of State, but the balance went to increase imports. If the increase of exports was due to a stimulus given by the fall in silver, we should expect to find that the percentage of silver imported after 1878-79 was larger than before. On the contrary, we find that from 1879-80 to 1884-85, as compared with the period from 1873-74 to 1878-79, a slightly less percentage of merchandise was imported, a

Nor during the period from 1879-80 to 1884-85.

considerably less percentage of silver was imported, and a larger percentage of gold was imported.

If we compare the period 1879-80 to 1884-85 with the period 1866-67 to 1872-73, before the fall in silver took place, we find that after the fall in silver a less percentage of both gold and silver was taken, and a higher percentage of merchandise. If we take the whole period 1873-74 to 1884-85 together, we find the percentages to be 83·8, 11·5, and 4·9 for merchandise, silver, and gold, respectively, and comparing these percentages with those for the period 1866-67 to 1872-73 (which are 78·3, 12·4, and 9·3), we find that after the rise in gold and fall in silver had come into operation, the imports into India were composed of a very much smaller proportion of gold, a slightly smaller proportion of silver, and a considerably larger proportion of merchandise. If India had been drained of her wealth by the large quantity of silver which she had to absorb during these years, it would have been found that she had largely increased, and not reduced, the proportion which her imports of silver bore to her imports of ordinary merchandise.

In face of these facts, we can only come to the conclusion that there has been no special drain of any magnitude on India owing to the depreciation of her currencey, because in fact her currency has not depreciated in relation to commodities. Prices have been maintained— nothing more.

Rate of increase in the value of the foreign trade of different countries measured by the standard of that country.

In connection with this matter I would call special attention to the very interesting table given in Appendix C, which I have taken from the recent Review of the Trade of British India for 1884-85, by Mr. J. E. O'Conor.

This table shows the rate of increase since 1873 of the value of the foreign trade of India and of certain other countries, which possess a gold standard, and, for facility of reference, I give here a summary of the results :—

Country.	Percentage of increase or decrease of foreign trade in 1884 as compared with 1873.		
	Imports.	Exports.	Total.
England	4·98	—8·71	—0·6
Italy	1·98*	4·44*	3·14*
France	27·32	—11·54	7·27
Germany	—13·11*	42·16*	7·89*
United States	3·98	43·55	21·4
India	68·04	51·21	57·49

To understand this table, we must recollect that India possesses a silver standard and the other countries a gold standard.

The silver prices of imports and exports have not risen in India, so that the table represents not merely the increase of the trade in value, but also in quantity. On the other hand, the prices of the imports and exports of the other countries, for which figures are given, have fallen because these prices are gold prices. The result has been that, although the quantity of the trade of gold countries has increased largely, the apparent value of that trade has increased very slightly, except in the case of the United States, because prices have fallen very nearly in proportion to the increase in trade.

---

* The figures are for 1883.

The partial de-
monetisat i o n
of silver has
prevented   a
fall in prices
in India.

In other words, the partial demonetisation of silver has given India stability of prices, while countries with a gold standard have ex perienced the evils of falling prices.

CHAPTER XXV.

EFFECTS OF THE FALL IN THE VALUE OF SILVER
AS COMPARED WITH GOLD ON INDIA.

In a country which is stationary as regards its economic conditions, and where consequently the increase of wealth and trade just keep pace with the increase of population, it will be obvious that a yearly increasing supply of the material of the standard is required, *cæteris paribus*, to prevent prices from falling. Population tends to grow in an increasing ratio, and the supply of the metal of the standard should follow the same ratio. If it does not do so, the increasing scarcity of coin, compared with the work which it is called upon to perform, must cause a fall in prices; and a fall of prices from this cause is necessarily attended with distress and economic disturbance.

An increasing supply of the precious metals necessary to prevent a fall in prices.

If the aggregate wealth and trade of a country are increasing more rapidly than population, a still further increase in the rate of production of the material composing the currency will be necessary to prevent prices from falling. The extension of civilisation to barbarous countries also creates a demand for special supplies of money to provide these countries with a currency, and to maintain and increase that currency in proportion to the increase of population, wealth, and trade.

Moreover, if labour becomes more efficient and commodities are more easily produced, it would probably be better for the world that there should be a corresponding increase in the production of the precious metals, so as to prevent the disturbance which accompanies a fall in prices, even when it is due to increased production of commodities.

Looking to the growth of population, the increase of trade and wealth, the extent to which uncivilised countries are being opened out, and the many improvements which are being made in the processes of manufacture, it will be obvious that a yearly increasing production of gold and silver is ordinarily required in order to maintain prices at the same level.

It has already been shown in Chapter XVI that, before the great gold discoveries, in the middle of the present century, prices had shown a marked tendency to fall. The gold discoveries of California and Australia reversed this tendency ; but to maintain prices at the level to which they then attained, it was necessary that the total production of gold should go on increasing year by year, or, if a bimetallic system were in force, that the total production of gold and silver should increase.

There has, however, been no such increase, nor, so far as can be foreseen, is there likely to be ; on the contrary, the production of gold has fallen off, and though the production of silver has increased, the abandonment of the bimetallic system has prevented the countries with a gold standard from reaping any of the benefits of this increase, and Mr. Giffen's conclusion that there will be a steady and progressive fall in prices all over the world appears to be unassailable.

The fall in gold prices after 1873 aggravated by the partial demonetisation of silver.

From the figures given on pages 69, 73, 78 and 79, we now know that a fall in prices was about to declare itself after 1873.

Up to that time gold and silver had divided between them the duty of money under a bi-metallic system which preserved the ratio of value between them at 1 to $15\frac{1}{2}$. After that year the bimetallic system was abandoned ; more work was thrown on gold and less on sil-ver,—the fall which would in any case have taken place in gold prices was aggravated by the partial demonetisation of silver, and the fall which would otherwise have taken place in silver prices was checked by the same cause.

If it be the case that the partial demonetisa-tion of silver did not depreciate that metal as compared with commodities, but merely obviat-ed an appreciation which was about to take place, then we cannot doubt that the silver countries have not lost by the demonetisation of silver, except in so far as they may have previously incurred liabilites in gold, or have found the operations of commerce hampered by the instability of the ratio between gold and silver, or been prevented from borrowing as cheaply as they otherwise might have done.

If the reduction of the proportion of duty as money which silver is required to perform has had the effect of maintaining silver prices at the same level, it might with much greater show of reason be argued that the silver coun-tries have gained rather than lost by the par-tial demonetisation of silver.

We have already seen that prices have fall-en steadily and heavily in countries with a gold standard, and that eminent authorities are of opinion that the fall is largely due to the in-creasing scarcity of gold in comparison with the work which it has to perform.

What, then, has been the effect on India ?

The figures given in pages 90, 97, and 100, show that exports from India have greatly increased since the fall in silver, but that the prices of these exports have not increased. In other words, India has not been drained of her wealth in consequence of the depreciation of the material of her currency.

Her increased exports are surplus wealth made available for export by improved communications, the opening of the Suez Canal, and the general reductions in freight. No special stimulus has been given to exports by a rise in silver prices; but the fall in the value of silver as compared with gold has obviated the decline which would otherwise have occurred, and has given India the advantage of stability of prices.

If the Indian currency had been depreciated, the silver prices of imports would have risen; as we have already seen, they have fallen rather than risen.

The partial demonetisation of silver was followed after an interval of a few years by good harvests in India, which were of special value to the country, because the cost of carriage both to the sea-coast and to Europe had been greatly cheapened, and a market was opened for surplus produce. The partial demonetisation of silver prevented that fall in prices which was otherwise inevitable, and India has consequently had the advantage for the last few years of good harvests, reduction in the cost of carriage, and fairly stable prices. If her trade is somewhat depressed at present, this is merely the reaction of the still greater depression in the countries with a gold standard.

With a view to show the general prosperity of India since the fall in the relative value of silver, I have selected a few articles which are not produced in India, and are not necessaries of life, in order to trace the course of imports of such articles since 1874-75 :—

Increased prosperity of India shown by the increased import of certain commodities.

Year. Average of five years ending	Clocks and Watches. Rs.	Corals. Rs.	Glass. Rs.	Matches. Rs.	Unwrought Copper. Rs.	Unwrought Tin. Rs.	Umbrellas. Rs.	Gold. Rs.	TOTAL. Rs.
1873-74 ...	3,27,000	5,45,000	18,38,000	4,25,000	30,82,000	11,29,000	10,46,000	3,14,36,000	3,98,28,000
1874-75 ...	3,77,000	6,71,000	31,89,000	5,85,000	22,80,000	13,41,000	11,94,000	2,08,92,000	3,04,79,000
1875-76 ...	4,38,000	8,14,000	34,99,000	6,70,000	38,72,000	16,18,000	19,64,000	1,83,64,000	3,12,39,000
1876-77 ...	3,57,000	7,24,000	28,04,000	7,66,000	47,96,000	17,86,000	13,67,000	1,44,37,000	2,70,37,000
1877-78 ...	4,19,000	7,00,000	29,14,000	9,98,000	51,69,000	22,12,000	18,85,000	1,57,89,000	3,00,86,000
1878-79 ...	4,83,000	8,19,000	31,87,000	8,64,000	46,51,000	15,08,000	23,80,000	1,46,30,000	2,85,22,000
1879-80 ...	5,42,000	12,38,000	32,93,000	9,65,000	57,17,000	9,84,000	20,40,000	2,05,04,000	3,52,83,000
1880-81 ...	8,20,000	13,76,900	38,02,000	10,15,000	42,04,000	17,68,000	27,29,000	3,67,21,000	5,34,35,000
1881-82 ...	1,32,000	18,54,000	45,48,000	14,44,000	44,88,000	16,93,000	20,96,000	4,85,64,000	6,55,19,000
1882-83 ...	9,24,000	19,59,000	84,37,000	17,44,000	53,93,000	27,64,000	23,28,000	5,09,51,000	7,08,99,000
1883-84 ...	10,34,000	23,12,000	56,01,003	13,57,000	68,74,000	23,47,000	27,60,000	5,46,95,000	7,69,80,000
1884-85 ...	9,45,000	18,25,000	49,97,000	20,43,000	62,11,000	22,18,000	33,53,000	4,77,82,000	6,93,74,000

Those who are familiar with the conditions of Indian life will know that the increased import of the articles shown in the table on p. 128 is the surest sign of Indian prosperity ; and the total increase in 1884-85 over the average of the five years ending 1873-74 is no less than 74 per cent. If gold, of which the price in silver has largely risen, be excluded, the increase is more than 157 per cent.

Instances might be multiplied to show the progress of India during the last twelve years ; but I will confine myself to one more table, showing the increase in the Excise and Stamp Revenue, the increase in the returns from the railways and canals constructed through the agency or on the financial reposibility of Government, and the growth of the cotton industry :—

Progress of certain heads of revenue and of the cotton industry.

	Excise.	Stamps.	Net return from Productive Public Works.	Number of spindles in cotton mills.
	Rs.	Rs.	Rs.	
1873-74...	2,28,76,800	2,69,99,360	—1,60,57,230	...
1874-75...	2,34,72,740	2,75,80,420	—1,43,61,080	...
1875-76 ..	2,49,43,390	2,83.53.680	—1,29,55,670	...
1876-77...	2,52,39.860	2,83,86,280	+ 68,91,530	1,231,284
1877-78 ..	2,45,80,290	2,99,34,830	— 45.63,290	1,289,706
1878-79 ..	2,61,93,490	3,11,05,400	—1,25,36,950	1,436,464
1879-80 ..	2,83,80,210	3,19,37,390	— 27,76,570	1,470,830
1880-81 ..	3,13,52,260	3,25,05,810	+ 12.23,490	1,471,730
1881-82 ..	3,42,72,740	3,38.13 720	+ 1,13,30,580	1,550,944
1882-83...	3,60,95,610	3,37,96,810	+ 48,23,530	1,654,108
1883-84...	3,83,69,610	3.51,32,010	+1,20.77,530	1,895,284
1884-85...	4,01,50,670	3,60,66,210	+ 80,30,334	2,047,801

The excise revenue has increased in 11 years by more than 75 per cent., and the stamp revenue by more than 33 per cent. The great railways and canals which are included under the head of Productive Public Works, appear to show an improvement of Rs. 2,40,87,564, but owing to the way in which the Indian accounts are kept, an adjustment is required on account of exchange, and if this be made, the real improvement is reduced to Rs. 1,54,00,000. The result is sufficiently remarkable if it be borne in mind that between 1873-74 and 1884-85 the Indian Government has been pressing on the construction of railways and canals, that many of these railways and canals are not yet in full working order, while others are under construction and swell the charge for interest, though not bringing in any revenue. The improvement in 1885-86 over 1873-74 will probably not be less than Rs. 2,00,00,000.

A large portion of the profits from the best paying lines is also absorbed by companies who undertook the construction of lines on a guarantee by Government, and the improvement which is shown above does not include the extra profits now received by these Companies. The Companies received in 1884-85 no less than Rs. 57,11,960 in addition to the guaranteed rate of interest of 5 per cent.

Rapid growth of Indian revenue since the fall in the value of silver relatively to gold.

Moreover, the progress of the Indian revenue shows that the general prosperity of the country, which is largely due to the stability of price maintained by the partial demonetisation of silver, very materially counterbalances, even from a purely financial point of view, the increasing burden thrown on the Government of India by the fall in the rate of exchange. For instance, the Indian Government set aside 150 lakhs of rupees in 1881 as a provision against future famine, and in 1882 remitted taxation to the amount, in round numbers, of 300 lakhs of rupees, thus disposing in all of 450 lakhs per annum.

At that time the rate of exchange was 1s. 1d. per rupee. It may possibly not be higher than 1s. 6d. per rupee in 1886-87,—a change which imposes an additional burden on Indian finance of nearly 200 lakhs of rupees. No additional taxation has been imposed since 1881, and the ordinary growth of Indian revenue since that date has been so rapid that, apart from the military expenditure which may be required on special grounds, 1 have little doubt that the revenue of 1886-87 will be found to balance the expenditure.

The fall in the rate of exchange cannot have had a ruinous influence on Indian finance, since the Government of India had surplus revenue of 450 lakhs per annum to dispose of in 1882, eight years after the fall began, and has since been able to meet all the ordinary cost of administration without additional taxation, although the further fall, subsequent to 1882, has thrown an additional burden on the finances of nearly 200 lakhs per annum.

CHAPTER XXVI.

UNIVERSAL BIMETALLISM.

Effect of the bimetallic system in checking the rise in prices after the great gold discoveries.

The general fall in prices which declared itself prior to 1848, and to which a reference was made on page 62, was checked by the increased production of gold, due to the discovery of gold mines in California and Australia. The production of gold was for some years seven-fold what the production had been before 1848, and a general rise in prices followed. At this time the bimetallic system was effectively maintained by France, and the rise in prices consequent on the gold discoveries was spread over the whole world, and was not confined to those countries only which had a gold standard. France gave up silver for export to the East, and absorbed gold in its place. The area of the employment of gold was in this way automatically extended, and that of the employment of silver contracted, so as to preserve a constant ratio of 1 to $15\frac{1}{2}$ between the market value of the two metals. I fall countries had been monometallic at that time, the rise in prices in countries with a gold standard would probably have been twice as great as it actually was, and there would have been little, if any, rise in prices in the silver countries. The market ratio between gold and silver might have become 1 to 12 or 1 to 10 instead of 1 to $15\frac{1}{2}$.

Aggregate production of gold and silver nearly the same since 1852.

The production of gold reached its highest point in a few years after the first discoveries; the alluvial deposits very soon began to be exhausted ; the production gradually fell off, and recourse to deep mining and expensive machinery became necessary. After a time, however, the annual production of silver began to increase; and, taking the two metals together, it may be said that there has been no very great variation in the total production since 1852.

In order to preserve stability of price, a yearly increasing production the material of the currency is required. It was therefore inevitable that, in face of the vastly increasing amount of work as money which gold and silver are called on to perform, there should be, sooner or later, a fall in price. It appears probable from the subsequent course of events that a fall in prices would have occurred in any case after 1873, but the fall in gold prices was aggravated by the action of Germany and France.

Total production of gold and silver not in excess of what is required.

Increased population, increased wealth, increased trade, and increased production, appear to have demanded, after 1873, the discovery of these new mines, at which, as Mr. Newmarch said, "the world ought to rejoice." Unfortunately no new mines of gold were discovered, and the partial demonetisation of silver at this time, and the abandonment of the bimetallic system, prevented the world from taking full advantage of the increased supplies of silver which were then coming into the market, and of which all nations would, under the bimetallic system, have reaped the full advantage without trouble and without thought.

At the very moment when the total supply of gold and silver was becoming insufficient for the demands of the world, the action of Germany and France deprived the gold-using coun-

Loss to gold countries caused by the abandonment of the bimetallic system in 1873.

tries of the benefits which they would have
received from the increased supplies of silver;
gold was called on to do the work of a still
wider area at the time when it was proving insufficient to keep up prices in the area hitherto
occupied. The result has been to aggravate
the inevitable fall of prices in gold countries, and
to obviate that fall in prices from which countries with a silver standard would otherwise
have suffered.

Question of gain or loss to India. India has suffered from the partial demonetisation of silver, because her obligations con-
tracted in gold now impose a heavier burden on
her than they otherwise would have done, because capitalists whose resources are in gold
hesitate to invest money in a country where the
standard is silver, and because an additional
element of uncertainty has been introduced into
all commercial transactions between silver and
gold-using countries. On the other hand, the
partial demonetisation of silver has prevented a
fall of prices in India, and has thereby conferred
a boon of immense value on the country. Grievous as is the burden which the so-called loss by
exchange imposes on Indian finance, and difficult
as it is for the Indian Government to recruit its
resources by additional taxation, I should, if
I were forced to strike a balance between the
gain and loss, hesitate to say that on the whole
India has, up to the present date, been a loser.

Universal bi-metallism required. The true remedy for a portion of the evils
from which the world now suffers is the adoption
of universal bimetallism at a fixed ratio to be
determined by mutual consent. What that
ratio should be, I shall not attempt to determine.

There is no magic in the ratio of 1 to 15½
rather than in 1 to 10 or 1 to 20. The loss of

the old ratio of 1 to 15½ was a terrible calamity, but the advantages of bimetallism will in the long run be obtained as satisfactorily under any other ratio which may be chosen by common consent.

The future ratio should be determined with reference to the circumstances of the time ; the benefits of that ratio, whatever it may be, will last for all time. The ratio of 1 to 15½ has tradition in its favour, and tradition is power- ful in a matter of this kind ; its adoption would redress some grievances which have been caused by the injustice of legislatures, and, what is the chief argument in its favour, it is probably the only ratio that would be accepted by nations, such as France, which hold a large amount of silver valued above the present market rate. I do not deny that the adoption of the ratio of 1 to 15½ instead of the present market ratio of 1 to 19 or 20 would involve loss to some and gain to other ; but to those who call Heaven to witness against such spoliation, I would reply that it was legislation that altered the ratio from 1 to 15½ ; that what legislation did legislation can undo ; and that the spoliation involved in going back to the ratio of 1 to 15½ would not be greater—nay, would be very much less—than the spoliation involved in passing from a ratio of 1 to 15½ to 1 to 19. On the other hand, it must be admitted that arguments of great weight can be advanced either for adopting the present market ratio as the future legal ratio, or for adopting a ratio somewhat higher than the present market ratio, but not so high as the old ratio of 1 to 15½. The ques- tion is one on which it would be useless to pronounce an opinion at the present time. The problem must, if a satisfactory solution is to be

Ratio between gold and silver should be fix- ed after consi- deration of the circum- stances of the time.

found, be approached in a spirit of conciliation, and the future welfare of the world depends very much more on the adoption of some fixed ratio rather than on the adoption of any particular ratio.

The choice of the world will probably fall on that ratio which will conciliate most interests and excite least opposition, but whatever ratio may be adopted, it should not be lower than the market ratio, nor higher than 1 to 15½. The longer the settlement of the question is delayed, the more difficult will it be to choose a ratio which will satisfy the interests of the nations concerned.

Future fall in prices probable. Even if a fixed ratio be established between gold and silver, it is more than probable that future years will see a fall in prices, though there may be a recovery from the present state of extreme depression.

The future may, however, be left to take care of itself; the world will not willingly accept the injustice which is involved in a progressive and continued fall in prices; and, no doubt, the increasing knowledge of mankind will lead to remedies being provided, which will, at any rate, alleviate the evils of a shrinking of the metallic currency in comparison with the work it has to do.

Possibility of the maintenance of the bimetallic system by a group of countries. Failing universal bimetallism, it would be desirable that bimetallism should be adopted by a group of countries sufficiently strong to maintain the fixed ratioy.

A statement prepared by the Director of the Mint of the United States shows that in 1884 France, Germany, and the United States held between them 1,793 millions of dollars in gold coin. It so happens that these countries and India hold the greater portion of the full legal tender silver coin of the world, and consequently if they adopted a bimetallic system, and India maintained her silver standard, they could not be exposed to an excessive drain of gold in exchange for silver.

Excluding India, France, Germany, and the United States, the rest of the civilised world holds only 440 millions of dollars in silver of full legal tender.

If, therefore, France, Germany, and the United States agreed to form a bimetallic union (India engaging to maintain the silver standard), they might in the most extreme case be offered 440 millions of silver dollars, taken from the currencies of other civilised nations in exchange for gold; but as they hold 1,793 millions of dollars in gold, their stock of gold could not possibly be exhausted, and they would, in accordance with the principles laid down in Chapter XI, have no difficulty in maintaining the fixed ratio.

There does not appear to be any likelihood that in the remote future the value of silver in relation to commodities will be depreciated below its present level, even if the bimetallic system be not adopted. On the contrary, looking to the wants of countries now only entering into the pale of civilisation, as well as of those which possess a forced paper currency, and to the probable increase of population and trade, we may reasonably anticipate that, whatever may be the future ratio of exchange between silver and gold, the former metal will rise in value relatively to commodities, or, in other

Improbability of the depreciation of silver in relation to commodities in the future.

words, that silver prices will in time tend towards a lower level.

If a fixed ratio between silver and gold be not adopted, gold prices will experience a still greater fall.

APPENDICES.

VARIATIONS IN THE WHOLESALE PRICES OF CERTAIN STAPLE

OF MARCH

EXPORTS.	1873. March.	1874. March.	1875. March.	1876. March.	1877. Jan. 4.
Castor oil (No. 1, fine pale)	100	101	85	...	111
Hides, buffalo, slaughtered, Patua ...	100	96	83	...	94
„ cow, slaughtered	100	106	97	...	96
Indigo, good	100	Nom.	...	Nom.	110
Jute, picked	100	137	132	128	150
„ ordinary	100	123	119	119	142
Lac dye, fine	100	...	73	45	69
„ middling	100	...	44	...	40
Shell lac, fine orange	100	149	...	102	68
„ middling	100	149	...	87	60
Linseed, fine, bold, clean	100	123	96	...	102
Rice, moonghy	100	153	Nil.	114	150
„ ballam	100	153	112	119	156
Saltpetre, 2-4 per cent. refraction ...	100	81	75	...	80
Seed, rape, yellow, mixed (2°/o) ...	100	89	83	...	104
„ til (black 4°/o)	100	97	84	...	105
„ poppy (3°/o)	100	95	73	...	81
Silk, raw, Cossimbazar	100	89	62	...	98
„ Gonatea	100	91	64	...	95
„ Juugypoor	100	86	62	...	95
„ Radhanagore...	100	87	59	.	96
„ Surdahs	100	87	60	...	100
Sugar, Benares	100	87	...	...	88
„ Date, Gurpatta	100	77	...	...	Nom.
„ Dulloah	100	...	...	86	Nom.
Tea, fine Pekeo	100	119	126	142	148
„ good Souchong	100	...	125	109	123
„ Congou	100	Nil.	...	112	119
Tobacco (Rungpore)	...	100	75	...	Nil.
Wheat, Doodiah	100	107	87	74	87

DIX A.

COMMODITIES OF EXPORT AT CALCUTTA ; TAKING THE PRICES
1873 AS-100.

1878.	1879.	1880.	1881.	1882.	1883.	1884.	1885.
January 10th.	January 9th.	January 13th.	January 4th.	January 7th.	January 15th.	January 14th.	January 5th.
115	119	99	83	...	81	87	79
75	69	96	93	83	87	71	...
72	90	95	95	97	103	100	101
88	114	112	105	117	107	117	103
...	153	169	156	137	96	162	110
149	142	163	144	130	87	155	101
58	54	73	49	39	27	Nil.	...
33	...	56	38	28	16	Nil.	...
49	63	157	124	93	80	98	56
44	58	157	113	84	75	91	53
106	Nom.	...	...	91	85	96	98
155	189	136	89	83	101	142	...
168	182	147	109	94	109	160	138
89	84	88	95	90	82	78	66
110	108	104	Nom.	...	93	107	87
128	122	119	98	88	102	109	Nil.
95	101	96	95	77	74	87	78
80	64	87	78	87	76	67	58
79	Nil.	91	75	Nil.	77	68	59
81	67	83	74	77	69	62	52
78	61	85	Nom.	Nil.	70	63	52
77	62	85	74	82	79	62	56
Nom.	Nil.	...	...	...	...	...	...
Nil.	84	113	92	95	97	87	Nil.
Nil.	110	133	127	113	107	...	Nil.
135	129	126	135	126	110	116	90
104	68	82	64	86	77	64	55
106	81	109	75	87	69	75	62
87	69	81	Nom.	...	...	125	94
109	109	...	91	96	84	75	72

APPENDIX B.

Pay of Postmen in India from 1855 to 1885.

Name of Post-office.	1855. Postmen.	1860. Postmen.	1865. Postmen.	1870. Postmen.	1875. Postmen.	1880. Postmen.	1885. Postmen.
Bengal.							
Calcutta ...	Rs. 15, 10, 8	Rs. 15, 10, 8	Rs. 15, 12, 10, 8	Rs. 15, 12, 10	Rs. 15, 12, 10	Rs. 15, 12, 10	Rs. 17, 13, 11
Dacca ...	„ 5	„ 5	„ 10, 5	„ 9 to 12, 6-8 to 9	„ 12, 9, 7-8	„ 15, 12	„ 15, 13
Patna ...	„ 6, 5	„ 10, 5	„ 10, 5	„ 9, 6-8	„ 9, 7-8, 7	„ 8, 7	„ 9, 7
Chyebassa ...	„ 5	„ 5	„ 5	„ 6-8	„ 7-8	„ 8	„ 9
Cuttack ...	„ 5	„ 5	„ 5	„ 6-8 to 9	„ 9, 7-8, 6	„ 9, 8	„ 10, 9
Assam.							
Gauhati ...	„ 5	„ 5	„ 6	„ 9 to 12	„ 10	„ 12, 10	„ 13, 11
Debrugarh ...	„ 5	„ 5	„ 6	„ 9 to 12	„ 10	„ 10, 8	„ 11

NAME OF POST-OFFICE.	1855. Postmen.	1860. Postmen.	1865. Postmen.	1870. Postmen.	1875. Postmen.	1880. Postmen.	1885. Postmen.
NORTH-WESTERN PROVINCES.							
Allahabad ...	Rs. 7, „ 5	Rs. 10, „ 6	Rs. 7, „ 6	Rs. 9 to 12, „ 6-8 to 9	Rs. 10, „ 9, „ 7-8, „ 6-8	Rs. 10, „ 9, „ 7-8, „ 6-8	Rs. 15, 11, 10, „ 7-8, 7, 6-8, „ 6
Aligarh ...	„ 5, „ 4	„ 5	„ 10	„ 9 to 12, „ 6-8 to 9	„ 10, „ 9, „ 7-8, „ 6-8	„ 10, „ 9, „ 7-8, „ 6-8	„ 11, „ 7-8, „ 6-8
Gorakhpur ...	„ 5	„ 5	„ 5	„ 9 to 12, „ 6-8 to 9	„ 10, „ 9, „ 7-8, „ 6-8	„ 10, „ 9, „ 7-8, „ 6-8	„ 10, „ 8-8, „ 8, „ 7-8, „ 7, „ 6-8
OUDH.							
Lucknow ...	„ 6, „ 5	„ 10, „ 6	„ 7, „ 6, „ 5	„ 9 to 12, „ 6-8 to 9	„ 10, „ 9, „ 7-8, „ 6-8	„ 10, „ 9, „ 7-8, „ 6-8	„ 10, „ 9, „ 8, „ 7
Fyzabad ...	„ 5	„ 6	„ 6	„ 9 to 12, „ 6-8 to 9	„ 10, „ 9, „ 7-8, „ 6-8	„ 10, „ 9, „ 7-8, „ 6-8	„ 10, „ 8, „ 7

Name of Post-office.	1855. Postmen.	1860. Postmen.	1865. Postmen.	1870. Postmen.	1875. Postmen.	1880. Postmen.	1885. Postmen.
PUNJAB.							
Lahore ...	...	{ Rs. 10 / " 6 }	Rs. 6	{ Rs. 9 to 12 / " 6-8 to 9 }	Rs. 9 / 8	Rs. 9 / " 8	{ Rs. 12 / " 8 / " 9 }
Peshawar ...	{ Rs. 10 / " 6 }	{ " 10 / " 6 }	{ " 10 / " 6 }	{ " 9 to 12 / " 6-8 to 9 }	" 9 / " 8	" 9 / " 8	{ " 10 }
Dehra Ghazi Khan ...	" 6	" 6	" 6	{ " 9 to 12 / " 6-8 to 9 }	" 8 / " 6-8	" 8 / " 6-8	{ " 9 / " 8 / " 6-8 }
SIND,							
Karachi ...	{ " 10 / " 7 }	{ 10 / " 7 / " 6 }	{ " 12 / " 9 }	{ " 9 to 12 / " 6-8 to 9 }	" 12 / 9	{ " 15 / " 12 / " 9 }	{ " 15 / " 13 / " 12 / " 11 }
Shikarpur ...	" 7	7	" 8	{ " 9 to 12 / " 6-8 to 9 }	" 10 / " 8	" 10 / " 8	" 12 / " 9
RAJPUTANA.							
Ajmere ...	" 3	{ 5 / 6 }	" 5	{ " 9 to 12 / " 6-8 to 9 }	" 10 / 0 / " 7-8 / " 6-8	" 10 / " 9 / " 7-8 / " 6-8	{ " 10 / " 9 / " 8 }
Mount Abu ...	" 6	" 6	" 6	" 6-8 to 9	" 9 / " 7-8	" 9 / " 7-8	" 10 / " 9

Name of Post-Office.	1855. Postmen.	1860. Postmen.	1865. Postmen.	1870. Postmen.	1875. Postmen.	1880. Postmen.	1885. Postmen.
Bombay.							
Bombay ...	Rs. 15, 10, 8	Rs. 15, 10, 8	Rs. 15, 12	Rs. 25 to 35, 17 to 23, 12 to 17	Rs. 28, 20, 14	Rs. 28, 20, 14	Rs. 28, 20, 14, 15, 10
Ahmedabad ...	„ 5	„ 5	„ 6	„ 9 to 12, 6-8 to 9	„ 10, 8	„ 10, 8	„ 11, 9, 8
Dhulia ...	„ 5	„ 5	„ 6	„ 9 to 12, 6-8 to 9	„ 10, 8	„ 10, 8	„ 11, 9
Ratnagiri ...	„ 5	„ 5	„ 6	„ 9 to 12, 6-8 to 9	„ 10, 8	„ 10, 8	„ 11, 9
Poona ...	„ 6, 5	„ 10, 6, 5	„ 10, 7	„ 9 to 12, 6-8 to 9	„ 12, 10	„ 15, 12, 10	„ 16, 13, 11
Dharwar ...	„ 6	„ 6	„ 6	„ 9 to 12, 6-8 to 9	„ 10, 8	„ 10, 8	„ 9, 11

B

APPENDIX B—*continued.*

Name of Post-office.	1855. Postmen.	1860. Postmen.	1865. Postmen.	1870. Postmen.	1875. Postmen.	1880. Postmen.	1885. Postmen.
Central India.							
Indore ...	Rs. 5	Rs. 10, „ 6	Rs. 10, „ 6	Rs. 9 to 12, „ 6-8 to 9	Rs. 10, „ 9, „ 7-8	Rs. 10, „ 9, „ 7-8	Rs. 11, „ 10, „ 9
Mhow ...	„ 5	„ 5	„ 6	„ 9 to 12, „ 6-8 to 9	„ 9, „ 7-8	„ 9, „ 7-8	„ 10, „ 9
Goona ...	„ 6	„ 5	„ 5	„ 6-8 to 9	„ 7-8, „ 6-8	„ 7-8, „ 6-8	„ 8
Nizam's Territory.							
Secunderabad ...	„ 6	„ 7, „ 6	„ 6	„ 9 to 12, „ 6-8 to 9	„ 9, „ 8, „ 7	„ 9, „ 8, „ 7, „ 6	„ 10, „ 9, „ 8
Central Provinces.							
Nagpur ...	„ 6, „ 6	„ 8, „ 6	„ 8, „ 6	„ 9 to 12, „ 6-8 to 9	„ 9, „ 7	„ 9, „ 7	„ 13, „ 10, „ 9, „ 8
Jubbulpur ...	„ 5	„ 5	„ 5	„ 9 to 12, „ 6-8 to 9	„ 9, „ 7	„ 9, „ 7	„ 13, „ 10, „ 9, „ 8

Name of Post-Office.	1855. Postmen.	1860. Postmen.	1865. Postmen.	1870. Postmen.	1875. Postmen.	1880. Postmen.	1885. Postmen.
Raipur ...	Rs. 6	Rs. 6	Rs. 6	{ Rs. 9 to 12 „ 6-8 to 9	Rs. 9 „ 7	Rs. 9 „ 7	Rs. 11 „ 9 „ 8
Sumbalpore ...	„ 5	„ 5	„ 5	„ 6-8 to 9	„ 7	„ 7	„ 10 „ 8
MADRAS.							
Madras ...	„ 15 „ 10 „ 9	Rs. 15 „ 12 „ 10 „ 8	„ 12 „ 10	„ 15 „ 13 „ 10 „ 8	Rs. 15 „ 12 „ 10	Rs. 15 „ 12 „ 10	„ 17 „ 14 „ 12
Bangalore ...	„ 7	„ 7	„ 7	„ 12 „ 9 to 12 „ 7 to 12	„ 12 „ 9 „ 8 „ 7	„ 12 „ 9 „ 8 „ 7	„ 13 „ 10 „ 9 „ 8
Tinnevelly ...	„ 4	„ 4	„ 4	„ 6-8 to 9	„ 7 „ 6	„ 7	„ 7 „ 6-8
Mangalore ...	„ 5-8	„ 5-8	„ 6	„ 9 to 12 „ 6-8 to 9	„ 9 „ 8 „ 7	„ 9 „ 8 „ 7	„ 10 „ 9 „ 8
Vizagapatam ...	„ 5-4	„ 5-4	„ 6	„ 9 to 12 „ 6-8 to 9	„ 9 „ 8 „ 7	„ 10 „ 8 „ 7	„ 11 „ 10 „ 9 „ 8

APPENDIX B—*continued.*

PAY OF POSTAL RUNNERS FROM 1855 TO 1885.

NAMES OF LINES.	1855.	1860.	1865.	1870.	1875.	1880.	1885.
BENGAL.							
Balasore to Cuttack ...	Rs. 4	Rs. 4	Rs. 3	Rs. 5	Rs. 5	{ Rs. 6 / ,, 5 }	Rs. 5
Dacca to Chittagong ...	,, 4	,, 4	,, 4	,, 5	,, 5	,, 5	,, 6
Cuttack to Angool (or Sumbalpur)	... 5	,, 3	,, 5	,, 5	,, 5	,, 5	,, 5
Purulia (Manbloom) to Chyebassa	,, 5	,, 4	,, 4	,, 4	,, 4	,, 3-8	,, 4-8
Gya to Nowrah ...	,, 4	,, 4	,, 4	,, 4	,, 4	...	...
Mozufferpur to Purneah ...	,, 3	,, 3	,, 3-8	,, 3-8	,, 3-8	,, 4	,, 5
Ranchi to Palamow ...	,, 2	,, 4	,, 4	,, 4	,, 4	,, 4	,, 5
OUDH AND NORTH-WESTERN PROVINCES.							
Lucknow to Sitapur ...	,, 4	,, 4	,, 4	,, 4	,, 4	,, 5	,, 4
Budaon to Bareilly ...	,, 3	,, 4	,, 4	,, 5	,, 4	,, 4	,, 4
Etawah to Mauipuri ...	,, 4	,, 4	,, 4	,, 4	,, 4	,, 4	...
Moradabad to Bijnur ...	,, 3	,, 4	,, 4	,, 4	,, 4	,, 4	,, 4
PUNJAB.							
Delhi (to all places) ...	,, 4	,, 4	,, 4	,, 5	,, 5	,, 5	,, 5
Jullundur to Hoshiarpur ...	,, 4	,, 4	,, 4	,, 4	,, 5	,, 5	,, 5
Kohat to Bunnoo or Edwardesabad ...	,, 4-8	,, 4	,, 4-8	,, 5	,, 5	,, 5	,, 5
Dehra Ginzi Khan to Dehra Ismail Khan	,, 4-8	,, 4	,, 4	,, 5	,, 5	,, 5	,, 5

PAY OF POSTAL RUNNERS FROM 1855 TO 1885.

NAMES OF LINES	1855.	1860.	1865.	1870.	1875.	1880.	1885.
SIND.							
Hyderabad to Mohad Khans Tando ...	Rs. 5	Rs. 5	Rs. 5	Rs. 4-8	Rs. 6	Rs. 6	Rs. 7
Jerruck to Tatta	...	...	,, 7	,, 7	,, 7	,, 7	,, 7
BOMBAY.							
Ratnagiri to Vingorla ...	...	,, 5	,, 6	,, 8	,, 7	,, 7	,, 7
Hubli to Harrihar ...	,, 5	,, 4	,, 6	,, 8	,, 7	,, 7	,, ... 6
Dhulia to Shirpur ...	,, 5	,, 5	,, 6	,, 8	,, 7	,, 7	,, 6
CENTRAL PROVINCES.							
Jubbulpur to Maudla ...	,, 5	...	,, 5	...	,, 5	,, 5	,, 5
MADRAS.							
Calicut to Tellichery ...	,, 4	,, 4	,, 5	,, 7	,, 7	,, 7	,, 7
Vizagapatam to Berhampur-Ganjam ...	...	,, 3-12	,, 5	,, 6	,, 6	,, 6	,, 6
MYSORE.							
Bangalore to Mysore ...	,, 4	,, 4	,, 4	,, 5	,, 6	,, 6	...
Average	Rs. 4·05	Rs. 4·56	Rs. 4·95	Rs. 5·2	Rs. 5·14	Rs. 5·24	Rs. 5·35

APPENDIX C.

000's omitted.

Year	ENGLAND Imports £	Exports £	Total £	FRANCE Imports £	Exports £	Total £	GERMANY Imports £	Exports £	Total £	ITALY Imports £	Exports £	Total £	UNITED STATES Imports £ (Year ended June 30)	Exports £	Total £	BRITISH INDIA Official Year	Imports £	Exports £	Total £
1873 ..	371,287	255,165	626,452	142,192	151,492	293,684	187,810	115,090	302,900	50,447	45,256	95,703	133,778	105,215	238,993	(1873-74)	31,629	53,114	84,743
1874 ..	370,053	239,558	609,641	140,308	148,044	288,352	180,285	117,655	297,890	51,826	39,128	90,954	118,200	118,632	236,841	(1874-75)	34,645	54,501	89,148
1875 ..	373,940	223,466	597,406	141,468	154,904	296,372	176,560	124,750	301,310	48,277	40,892	89,169	111,043	104,017	215,060	(1875-76)	37,113	56,212	93,325
1876 ..	375,155	200,039	575,794	150,536	143,024	302,560	199,105	127,385	317,490	52,283	48,340	100,623	95,088	109,406	205,484	(1876-77)	35,367	58,930	94,297
1877 ..	394,419	198,843	593,262	146,792	137,452	284,244	188,710	138,120	326,830	45,662	37,369	83,021	94,026	122,848	216,874	(1877-78)	39,326	63,144	102,470
1878 ..	368,771	192,849	561,620	167,048	127,188	294,236	175,685	144,357	320,042	42,359	39,944	82,302	91,052	141,814	232,866	(1878-79)	36,506	58,708	95,274
1879 ..	362,992	191,532	554,524	183,603	129,252	313,060	188,670	138,785	327,455	49,881	42,870	92,751	92,870	145,488	238,358	(1879-80)	39,742	64,951	104,693
1880 ..	411,230	223,060	634,290	201,828	138,716	340,044	141,835	144,770	285,805	47,447	44,139	91,586	130,157	171,655	310,812	(1880-81)	50,309	71,974	122,283
1881 ..	397,022	234,023	631,045	194,536	142,460	336,996	148,150	143,850	297,000	49,548	46,574	96,122	133,889	184,151	318,040	(1881-82)	46,902	79,255	120,247
1882 ..	415,020	241,467	654,487	192,872	142,976	335,848	156,475	159,525	316,000	49,039	45,983	95,022	150,907	152,758	303,725	(1882-83)	50,003	80,508	130,601
1883 ..	426,892	239,799	666,691	192,172	138,075	330,247	163,185	163,610	326,795	51,449	47,294	98,712	150,663	167,546	318,209	(1883-84)	52,704	85,008	137,712
1884 ..	389,775	232,928	622,703	181,039	134,004	315,043	..	..	..	..	..	..	139,104	151,034	290,138	(1884-85)	53,149	80,313	133,462
Percentage of increase or decrease in 1884 as compared with 1873..	+4·98	-8·71	-0·6	+27·32	-11·54	+7·27	-13·11*	+42·16*	+7·89*	+1·93*	+4·44*	+3·14*	+3·98	+43·55	+21·4		+68·04	+51·21	+57·49

* Increase in 1883.

www.ingramcontent.com/pod-product-compliance
Lightning Source LLC
Chambersburg PA
CBHW020549270326
41927CB00006B/771